sweet
comfort food

glorious desserts and treats like mother used to make

sweet
comfort food

glorious desserts and treats like mother used to make

Over 70 irresistible
home-cooked sweets shown
step-by-step with 300 colour
photographs – from timeless
childhood favourites to totally
outrageous indulgences

contributing editor: bridget jones

southwater

This edition is published by Southwater

Southwater is an imprint of Anness Publishing Ltd
Hermes House, 88–89 Blackfriars Road, London SE1 8HA
tel. 020 7401 2077; fax 020 7633 9499
www.southwaterbooks.com; info@anness.com

© Anness Publishing Ltd 2006

UK agent: The Manning Partnership Ltd
6 The Old Dairy, Melcombe Road, Bath BA2 3LR
tel. 01225 478444; fax 01225 478440; sales@manning-partnership.co.uk

UK distributor: Grantham Book Services Ltd
Isaac Newton Way, Alma Park Industrial Estate, Grantham, Lincs NG31 9SD
tel. 01476 541080; fax 01476 541061; orders@gbs.tbs-ltd.co.uk

North American agent/distributor: National Book Network
4501 Forbes Boulevard, Suite 200, Lanham, MD 20706
tel. 301 459 3366; fax 301 429 5746; www.nbnbooks.com

Australian agent/distributor: Pan Macmillan Australia
Level 18, St Martins Tower, 31 Market St, Sydney, NSW 2000
tel. 1300 135 113; fax 1300 135 103; customer.service@macmillan.com.au

New Zealand agent/distributor: David Bateman Ltd
30 Tarndale Grove, Off Bush Road, Albany, Auckland; tel. (09) 415 7664; fax (09) 415 8892

Publisher: Joanna Lorenz
Editorial director: Helen Sudell
Editors: Simona Hill and Elizabeth Woodland
Recipes: Catherine Atkinson, Mary Banks, Alex Barker, Judy Bastyra, Angela Boggiano,
Maxine Clark, Roz Denny, Joanna Farrow, Jennie Fleetwood, Brian Glover, Nicola Graimes,
Deh-ta Hsuing, Christine Ingram, Becky Johnson, Lucy Knox, Sally Mansfield, Christine
McFadden, Jane Milton, Sallie Morris, Keith Richmond, Jenni Shapter, Marlena Spieler,
Liz Trigg, Jenny White, Kate Whiteman, Lucy Whiteman, Jeni Wright.
Home economists: Eliza Baird, Alex Barker, Caroline Barty, Joanna Farrow, Annabel Ford,
Christine France, Carole Handslip, Kate Jay, Becky Johnson, Jill Jones, Bridget Sargeson,
Jennie Shapter, Carol Tennant, Sunil Vijayakar, Jenny White.
Stylists: Nicki Dowey, Penny Markham, Lucy McKelvie, Marion Price, Helen Trent, Linda Tubby.
Photographers: Frank Adam, Tim Auty, Martin Brigdale, Louisa Dare, Nicki Dowey, Gus Filgate,
John Heseltine, Amanda Heywood, Janine Hosegood, Dave King, William Lingwood,
Thomas Odulate, Craig Roberson, Simon Smith, Sam Stowell.
Designer: Design Principals
Cover designer: Balley Design Associates
Production controller: Claire Rae

Previously published as part of a larger volume, *Best-Ever Comfort Food*

10 9 8 7 6 5 4 3 2 1

NOTES

Bracketed terms are intended for American readers.

For all recipes, quantities are given in both metric and imperial measures and,
where appropriate, measures are also given in standard cups and spoons.
Follow one set, but not a mixture, because they are not interchangeable.
Standard spoon and cup measures are level.
1 tsp = 5ml, 1 tbsp = 15ml, 1 cup = 250ml/8fl oz

Australian standard tablespoons are 20ml. Australian readers should use 3 tsp in place
of 1 tbsp for measuring small quantities of gelatine, flour, salt, etc.

Medium (US large) eggs are used unless otherwise stated.

The nutritional analysis given for each recipe is calculated per portion (i.e. serving or item),
unless otherwise stated. If the recipe gives a range, such as Serves 4–6, then the analysis
will be for the larger portion size. The anaylsis does not include unmeasured ingredients,
such as sugar added to taste, or accompaniments such as cream.

Front cover shows Iced Tiramisù – for recipe, see page 15.

Contents

Introduction   6

Chill-out Desserts   8

Hot Puddings, Desserts and Drinks   28

Teatime Treats, Cakes and Breads   62

Index   96

INTRODUCTION

Sweet food is one of life's great pleasures, so why not treat yourself to an indulgent dessert or ice cream? It is the perfect way to finish a meal with family and friends, and is ideal for days off, when you only have yourself to please.

We all have our favourite comfort foods – they might be creamy, sweet, fruity, hot or cold, and they appeal directly to our body's feel-good responses. Foods that we enjoy eating often have pleasant associations and are hard to resist. Our favourite dishes might be based on childhood memories of times when we felt safe and secure, enjoyable trips abroad, or special celebration treats. Eating pleasurable food is deeply satisfying; it relieves us of our hunger and makes us feel content. When our hunger is satisfied after a meal that we have enjoyed, all is well with our world. We have revived our blood-sugar levels to an even balance, and our mood is restored to good humour.

Many favourite comfort foods are simple offerings that are not difficult to make: a thick slab of moist cake with a mug of strong coffee; a fruity summer pudding; a cool, classic ice cream; or home-baked cookies dunked in a cup of tea. With ease of cooking in mind, all of the recipes in this book are no-fuss, everyday recipes, made with ingredients that are readily available. None of them involve complicated cooking methods, though some do take time to cook. What they have in common is an appeal to a basic instinct in all of us. Food nurtures the body and nourishes the soul. Eating is essential, and we all enjoy good, flavourful food, whether alone or in company. To that end, here is a divine collection of over 70 appealing, tried-and-tested dessert recipes from all over the world.

Comfort food does not necessarily mean unhealthy eating, although some of these recipes might best be kept as extra special treats. It's really about unhurried

Above: Nothing beats the comforting simplicity of ice cream. Adding fresh chocolate sauce to the mixture has allowed this dessert to stay soft, even after freezing.

planning, choosing familiar ingredients, pleasurable shopping trips and effortless food preparation. Food at its best is always home-made, and knowing it's been made using the freshest ingredients, just before it's about to be consumed, adds to our nurturing instincts.

Enjoying food and its different aromas, tastes and textures, and learning to cook the foods that we take pleasure in eating should be habit-forming. With so many indulgent recipes at your disposal, and suggestions for every dessert imaginable, you should never be stuck for sweet ideas again.

Right: Sweet and sugary foods are comforting. They taste good and provide instant life to flagging energy levels. Fresh home-baked cakes taste better and will keep you feeling fuller for longer than store-bought confectionery.

Left: Chelsea buns make the perfect accompaniment to a cup of coffee or tea; serve warm for a tasty treat.

Chill-out
Desserts

Ice cream is a perennial favourite with children,
and for many of us that never changes. More
grown-up, but just as irresistible, are lavish
mousses, gooey chilled pies, and creamy creations
with fresh fruit and lashings of chocolate.

CLASSIC VANILLA ICE CREAM

NOTHING BEATS THE COMFORTING SIMPLICITY OF VANILLA ICE CREAM FOR EVOKING CHILDHOOD MEMORIES. VANILLA PODS ARE WELL WORTH BUYING FOR THE SUPERB FLAVOUR THEY IMPART.

SERVES FOUR

INGREDIENTS

1 vanilla pod (bean)
300ml/½ pint/1¼ cups semi-skimmed milk
4 egg yolks
75g/3oz/6 tbsp caster (superfine) sugar
5ml/1 tsp cornflour (cornstarch)
300ml/½ pint/1¼ cups double (heavy) cream

COOK'S TIP
Don't throw the vanilla pod away after use. Instead, rinse it in cold water, dry and store in the sugar jar. After a week or so the sugar will take on the wonderful aroma and flavour of the vanilla and will be delicious sprinkled over summer fruits. Use it to sweeten whipped cream, custard, biscuits and shortbread.

1 Using a small knife, slit the vanilla pod lengthways. Pour the milk into a heavy pan, add the vanilla pod and bring to the boil. Remove from the heat and leave for 15 minutes to allow the flavours to infuse.

2 Lift the vanilla pod up. Holding it over the pan, scrape the black seeds out of the pod with a small knife so that they fall back into the milk. Set the vanilla pod aside and bring the milk back to the boil.

3 Whisk the egg yolks, sugar and cornflour in a bowl until the mixture is thick and foamy. Gradually pour on the hot milk, whisking constantly. Return the mixture to the pan and cook over a gentle heat, stirring all the time.

VARIATION
If you are using an ice cream maker: Stir the cream into the custard and churn the mixture until thick.

4 When the custard thickens and is smooth, pour it back into the bowl. Cool it, then chill.

5 Whip the cream until it has thickened but still falls from a spoon. Fold it into the custard and pour into a plastic tub or similar freezerproof container. Freeze for 6 hours or until firm enough to scoop, beating twice with a fork, or in a food processor.

6 Scoop into dishes, bowls or bought cones – or eat straight from the tub.

Energy 542Kcal/2245kJ; Protein 6.8g; Carbohydrate 24.4g, of which sugars 24.4g; Fat 47.1g, of which saturates 27.4g; Cholesterol 309mg; Calcium 160mg; Fibre 0g; Sodium 59mg.

CHOCOLATE RIPPLE ICE CREAM

THIS CREAMY, DARK CHOCOLATE ICE CREAM, UNEVENLY RIPPLED WITH WONDERFUL SWIRLS OF RICH CHOCOLATE SAUCE, WILL STAY DELICIOUSLY SOFT EVEN AFTER FREEZING. NOT THAT IT WILL REMAIN IN THE FREEZER FOR LONG — IT IS PERFECT FOR CELEBRATIONS AS WELL AS TIMES OF GREATEST NEED!

SERVES FOUR TO SIX

INGREDIENTS
   4 egg yolks
   75g/3oz/6 tbsp caster (superfine)
     sugar
   5ml/1 tsp cornflour (cornstarch)
   300ml/½ pint/1¼ cups
     semi-skimmed milk
   250g/9oz dark (bittersweet)
     chocolate, broken
     into squares
   25g/1oz/2 tbsp butter, diced
   30ml/2 tbsp golden (light corn) syrup
   90ml/6 tbsp single (light) cream or
     cream and milk mixed
   300ml/½ pint/1¼ cups whipping
     cream
   wafer biscuits, to serve

1 Put the yolks, sugar and cornflour in a bowl and whisk until thick and foamy. Pour the milk into a pan, bring it just to the boil, then gradually pour it on to the yolk mixture, whisking constantly.

2 Return the mixture to the pan and cook over a gentle heat, stirring constantly until the custard thickens and is smooth. Pour it back into the bowl and stir in 150g/5oz of the chocolate until melted. Cover the chocolate custard closely, leave it to cool, then chill.

3 Put the remaining chocolate into a pan and add the butter. Spoon in the golden syrup. Heat gently, stirring, until the chocolate and butter have melted.

4 Stir in the single cream or cream and milk mixture. Heat gently, stirring continuously, until the mixture is smooth, then leave this chocolate sauce to cool, stirring occasionally.

5 Whip the cream until it has thickened, but is still soft enough to fall from a spoon. Fold it into the custard, pour into a plastic tub or similar freezerproof container and freeze for 5 hours until thick, beating once with a fork or electric whisk or in a food processor. Beat the ice cream in the tub one more time.

6 Add alternate spoonfuls of ice cream and chocolate sauce to a 1.5 litre/ 2½ pint/6¼ cup plastic container. Freeze for 5–6 hours until firm. Serve with wafers. Using an ice cream maker: Stir the cream into the custard and churn for 20–25 minutes until thick.

Energy 900Kcal/3749kJ; Protein 11g; Carbohydrate 74.9g, of which sugars 74.3g; Fat 63.9g, of which saturates 37.8g; Cholesterol 314mg; Calcium 211mg; Fibre 1.6g; Sodium 142mg.

ICED RASPBERRY AND ALMOND TRIFLE

THIS DELICIOUS COMBINATION OF ALMONDY SPONGE, SHERRIED FRUIT, ICE CREAM AND MASCARPONE IS SHEER INDULGENCE FOR TRIFLE LOVERS. THE SPONGE AND TOPPING CAN BE MADE A DAY IN ADVANCE AND THE ASSEMBLED TRIFLE WILL SIT HAPPILY IN THE REFRIGERATOR FOR AN HOUR BEFORE SERVING.

SERVES EIGHT TO TEN

INGREDIENTS
- 115g/4oz/½ cup unsalted (sweet) butter, softened
- 115g/4oz/½ cup light muscovado (brown) sugar
- 2 eggs
- 75g/3oz/⅔ cup self-raising (self-rising) flour
- 2.5ml/½ tsp baking powder
- 115g/4oz/1 cup ground almonds
- 5ml/1 tsp almond extract
- 15ml/1 tbsp milk

To finish
- 300g/11oz/scant 2 cups raspberries
- 50g/2oz/½ cup flaked (sliced) almonds, toasted
- 90ml/6 tbsp fresh orange juice
- 200ml/7fl oz/scant 1 cup medium sherry
- 500g/1¼lb/2½ cups mascarpone cheese
- 150g/5oz/⅔ cup Greek (US strained plain) yogurt
- 30ml/2 tbsp icing (confectioners') sugar
- about 250ml/8fl oz/1 cup vanilla ice cream
- about 250ml/8fl oz/1 cup raspberry ice cream or sorbet

VARIATION
The trifle is equally delicious made with other fresh fruits, such as strawberries, grapes, or chopped peached – or a mixture of fruits.

1 Preheat the oven to 180°C/350°F/ Gas 4. Grease and line a 20cm/8in round cake tin. Put the butter, sugar, eggs, flour, baking powder, almonds and almond extract in a large bowl and beat with an electric whisk for 2 minutes until creamy. Stir in the milk.

2 Spoon the mixture into the prepared tin, level the surface and bake for about 30 minutes or until just firm in the centre. Transfer to a wire rack and leave to cool.

3 Cut the sponge into chunky pieces and place these in the base of a 1.75 litre/3 pint/7½ cup glass serving dish. Scatter with half the raspberries and almonds. Mix the orange juice with 90ml/6 tbsp of the sherry.

4 Spoon over the orange and sherry mixture. Beat the mascarpone in a bowl with the yogurt, icing sugar and remaining sherry. Put the trifle dish and the mascarpone in the refrigerator until you are ready to assemble the trifle.

5 To serve, scoop the ice cream and sorbet into the trifle dish. Reserve a few of the remaining raspberries and almonds for the decoration, then scatter the rest over the ice cream. Spoon over the mascarpone mixture and scatter with the reserved raspberries and almonds. Chill the trifle for up to 1 hour before serving.

Energy 608Kcal/2537kJ; Protein 17.2g; Carbohydrate 41.9g, of which sugars 33.7g; Fat 39.4g, of which saturates 18.1g; Cholesterol 134mg; Calcium 357mg; Fibre 2.8g; Sodium 269mg.

CHOCOLATE, RUM AND RAISIN ROULADE

THIS RICH DESSERT TREAT CAN BE MADE AND FROZEN WELL IN ADVANCE. IF IT IS SLICED BEFORE FREEZING, SINGLE SLICES MAKE EXCELLENT IMPROMPTU PICK-ME-UPS. USE VANILLA, CHOCOLATE OR COFFEE ICE CREAM IF YOU PREFER — ALL VERSIONS WILL BE JUST AS ENJOYABLY INDULGENT.

SERVES SIX

INGREDIENTS

   115g/4oz plain (semisweet)
      chocolate, broken into pieces
   4 eggs, separated
   115g/4oz/generous ½ cup
      caster (superfine) sugar
   cocoa powder and icing
      (confectioners') sugar, for dusting
For the filling
   150ml/¼ pint/⅔ cup double (heavy)
      cream
   15ml/1 tbsp icing (confectioners')
      sugar
   30ml/2 tbsp rum
   300ml/½ pint/1¼ cups rum and
      raisin ice cream

1 Make the roulade. Preheat the oven to 180°C/350°F/Gas 4. Grease a 33 x 23cm/13 x 9in Swiss roll tin (jelly roll pan) and line with non-stick baking parchment. Grease the parchment. Melt the chocolate in a heatproof bowl set over a pan of simmering water.

2 In a separate bowl, whisk the egg yolks with the caster sugar until thick and pale. Stir the melted chocolate into the yolk mixture. Whisk the egg whites in a grease-free bowl until stiff. Stir a quarter of the whites into the yolk mixture to lighten it, then fold in the remainder.

3 Pour the mixture into the prepared tin and spread it gently into the corners. Bake for about 20 minutes until the cake has risen and is just firm. Turn it out on to a sheet of greaseproof paper which has been supported on a baking sheet and generously dusted with caster sugar. Leave to cool, then peel away the lining paper.

4 Make the filling. Whip the cream with the icing sugar and rum until it forms soft peaks, then spread the mixture to within 1cm/½in of the edges of the sponge. Freeze for 1 hour.

5 Using a dessertspoon, scoop up long curls of the ice cream and lay an even layer over the cream.

6 Starting from a narrow end, carefully roll up the sponge, using the paper to help. Slide the roulade off the paper-lined baking sheet and on to a long plate that is freezerproof. Cover and freeze overnight. Transfer to the fridge 30 minutes before serving. Serve dusted with cocoa powder and icing sugar.

Energy 474Kcal/1982kJ; Protein 8.3g; Carbohydrate 47.5g, of which sugars 46.1g; Fat 27.5g, of which saturates 16g; Cholesterol 203mg; Calcium 117mg; Fibre 0.5g; Sodium 99mg.

ZABAGLIONE ICE CREAM TORTE

FOR ANYONE WHO LIKES ZABAGLIONE, THE FAMOUS, WHISKED ITALIAN DESSERT, THIS SIMPLE ICED VERSION IS AN ABSOLUTE MUST! ITS TASTE AND TEXTURE ARE JUST AS GOOD, AND THERE'S NO LAST-MINUTE WHISKING TO WORRY ABOUT.

SERVES TEN

INGREDIENTS
175g/6oz amaretti biscuits
115g/4oz/½ cup ready-to-eat dried
   apricots, finely chopped
65g/2½oz/5 tbsp unsalted (sweet)
   butter, melted
For the ice cream
65g/2½oz/5 tbsp light muscovado
   (brown) sugar
75ml/5 tbsp water
5 egg yolks
250ml/8fl oz/1 cup double (heavy)
   cream
75ml/5 tbsp Madeira or cream sherry
For the apricot compote
150g/5oz/generous ½ cup ready-to-
   eat dried apricots
25g/1oz/2 tbsp light muscovado sugar
150ml/½ pint/⅔ cup water

1 Put the biscuits in a strong plastic bag and crush with a rolling pin. Place in a bowl and stir in the apricots and melted butter until evenly combined.

2 Using a dampened dessertspoon, pack the mixture evenly on to the bottom and up the sides of a 24cm/9½in loose-based flan tin (tart pan) about 4cm/1½in deep. Chill.

3 Make the ice cream. Put the sugar and water in a small, heavy pan and heat, stirring, until the sugar dissolves. Bring to the boil and boil for 2 minutes without stirring. Heat a large pan of water to simmering. Put the egg yolks in a large bowl that fits on the pan.

4 Off the heat, whisk the egg yolks until pale, then gradually whisk in the sugar syrup. Put the bowl over the pan of simmering water and continue to whisk for about 10 minutes or until the mixture is thick and pale, and holds the trail of the whisk when it is lifted out of the mixture.

5 Remove the bowl from the heat and carry on whisking for a further 5 minutes or until the mixture is cold. In a separate bowl, whip the cream with the Madeira or sherry until it stands in peaks.

6 Using a large metal spoon, fold the cream into the whisked mixture. Spoon it into the biscuit case, level the surface, cover and freeze overnight.

7 To make the compote, simmer the apricots and sugar in the water until the apricots are plump and the juices are syrupy, adding a little more water if necessary. Leave to cool and then chill.

8 Serve the torte in slices with a little of the compote spooned over, or to one side of, each portion.

Energy 367Kcal/1530kJ; Protein 4g; Carbohydrate 33.9g, of which sugars 26.3g; Fat 24g, of which saturates 13.6g; Cholesterol 149mg; Calcium 73mg; Fibre 1.9g; Sodium 112mg.

ICED TIRAMISÙ

THE TITLE OF THIS FAVOURITE ITALIAN DESSERT MEANS "PICK-ME-UP", WHICH IS PROBABLY LARGELY TO DO WITH THE GENEROUS QUANTITY OF ALCOHOL THAT IS SO OFTEN THROWN IN. THE TRADITIONAL DESSERT IS NOT FROZEN BUT IT IS FABULOUS IN THIS GUISE, EVEN MADE WITH LIGHT FROMAGE FRAIS.

SERVES FOUR

INGREDIENTS

150g/5oz/¾ cup caster (superfine) sugar
150ml/¼ pint/⅔ cup water
250g/9oz/generous 1 cup mascarpone
200g/7oz/scant 1 cup virtually fat-free fromage frais or ricotta
5ml/1 tsp vanilla extract
10ml/2 tsp instant coffee, dissolved in 30ml/2 tbsp boiling water
30ml/2 tbsp coffee liqueur or brandy
75g/3oz sponge finger biscuits
cocoa powder, for dusting
chocolate curls, to decorate

1 Put 115g/4oz/½ cup of the sugar into a small pan. Add the water and bring to the boil, stirring until the sugar has dissolved. Leave the syrup to cool, then chill it.

4 Meanwhile, put the instant coffee mixture in a small bowl, sweeten with the remaining sugar, then add the liqueur or brandy. Stir well and leave to cool.

5 Crumble the biscuits into small pieces and toss them in the coffee mixture. If you have made the ice cream by hand, beat it again.

6 Spoon a third of the ice cream into a 900ml/1½ pint/3¾ cup plastic container, spoon over half the biscuits then top with half the remaining ice cream.

7 Sprinkle over the last of the coffee-soaked biscuits, then cover with the remaining ice cream. Freeze for 2–3 hours until firm enough to scoop. Dust with cocoa powder and spoon into glass dishes. Decorate with chocolate curls, and serve.

2 Put the mascarpone into a bowl. Beat it with a spoon until it is soft, then stir in the fromage frais or ricotta. Add the chilled sugar syrup, a little at a time, then stir in the vanilla essence.

3 By hand: Spoon the mixture into a plastic tub or similar freezerproof container and freeze for 4 hours, beating once with a fork, electric mixer or in a food processor to break up the ice crystals.

VARIATION

If you are using an ice cream maker: Churn the mascarpone mixture until it is thick but too soft to scoop.

Energy 323Kcal/1367kJ; Protein 11.8g; Carbohydrate 53.8g, of which sugars 49.6g; Fat 8.3g, of which saturates 4.7g; Cholesterol 74mg; Calcium 228mg; Fibre 0.2g; Sodium 97mg.

MARBLED CHOCOLATE CHEESECAKE

BAKED CHEESECAKE IS PLEASING TO PREPARE AND THIS CHOCOLATE-VANILLA COMBO IS SUPERLATIVE.

SERVES SIX

INGREDIENTS

   50g/2oz/½ cup unsweetened
    cocoa powder
   900g/2lb cream cheese,
    at room temperature
   200g/7oz/scant 1 cup caster
    (superfine) sugar
   4 eggs
   5ml/1 tsp vanilla extract
   75g/3oz digestive biscuits (graham
    crackers), crushed

1 Preheat the oven to 180°C/350°F/Gas 4.

2 Line a 20 x 8 cm/8 x 3in cake tin (pan) with baking parchment. Grease the paper.

3 Sift the cocoa powder into a bowl. Add 75ml/5tbsp hot water and stir until mixed and smooth.

4 Beat the cheese until smooth, then beat in the sugar, followed by the eggs, one at a time. Do not overmix. Divide the mixture evenly between two bowls. Stir the chocolate mixture into one bowl, then add the vanilla extract to the remaining mixture.

5 Pour a cup or ladleful of the plain mixture into the centre of the tin; it will spread out into an even layer. Slowly pour over a cupful of chocolate mixture in the centre. Continue to alternate the cake mixtures in this way until both are used up. Draw a thin metal skewer through the cake mixture for a marbled effect.

6 Set the tin in a roasting pan and pour in hot water to come 4cm/1½in up the sides of the cake tin.

7 Bake the cheesecake for about 1½ hours, until the top is golden. (The cake will rise during baking and sink later.) Cool in the tin on a wire rack.

8 Run a knife around the inside edge of the cake. Invert a flat plate over the tin and turn out the cake.

9 Sprinkle the crushed biscuits evenly over the cheesecake. Gently invert another plate on top, and turn both cake and plates over again. Cover and place in the refrigerator for at least 3 hours, preferably overnight.

Energy 933Kcal/3869kJ; Protein 12.2g; Carbohydrate 44.4g, of which sugars 36.5g; Fat 80g, of which saturates 48g; Cholesterol 300mg; Calcium 210mg; Fibre 1.3g; Sodium 662mg.

LEMON CHEESECAKE WITH FOREST FRUITS

THIS ZESTY CHEESECAKE HAS A LIGHT CORNFLAKE BASE AND A COLOURFUL TOPPING OF LUSCIOUS, FOREST FRUITS. IT IS THE PERFECT REVIVER — SLIGHTLY NAUGHTY BUT FULL OF GOOD INGREDIENTS.

SERVES EIGHT

INGREDIENTS
  50g/2oz/¼ cup unsalted
    (sweet) butter
  25g/1oz/2 tbsp soft light brown sugar
  45ml/3 tbsp golden (light corn) syrup
  115g/4oz/generous 1 cup cornflakes
  11g/¼oz sachet powdered gelatine
  225g/8oz/1 cup soft cheese
  150g/5oz/generous ½ cup Greek (US
    strained plain) yogurt
  150ml/¼ pint/⅔ cup single
    (light) cream
  finely grated rind and juice of
    2 lemons
  75g/3oz/6 tbsp caster
    (superfine) sugar
  2 eggs, separated
  225g/8oz/2 cups mixed, prepared
    fresh forest fruits, such as
    blackberries, raspberries and
    redcurrants, to decorate
  icing (confectioners') sugar,
    for dusting

1 Place the butter, brown sugar and syrup in a pan and heat over a low heat, stirring, until the mixture has melted and is well blended. Remove from the heat and stir in the cornflakes.

2 Press the mixture over the base of a deep 20cm/8in loose-based round cake tin (pan). Chill for 30 minutes.

VARIATION
Use unsweetened puffed rice cereal or rice crispies in place of the cornflakes.

3 Sprinkle the gelatine over 45ml/ 3 tbsp water in a bowl and leave to soak for a few minutes. Place the bowl over a pan of simmering water and stir until the gelatine has dissolved. Place the cheese, yogurt, cream, lemon rind and juice, caster sugar and egg yolks in a large bowl and beat until smooth and thoroughly mixed.

4 Add the hot gelatine to the cheese and lemon mixture and beat well.

5 Whisk the egg whites until stiff, then fold into the cheese mixture.

6 Pour the cheese mixture over the cornflake base and level the surface. Chill for 4–5 hours, or until the filling has set.

7 Carefully remove the cheesecake from the tin and place on a serving plate. Decorate with the mixed fresh fruits, dust with icing sugar and serve.

Energy 340Kcal/1422kJ; Protein 7.7g; Carbohydrate 32.5g, of which sugars 20.8g; Fat 21.1g, of which saturates 12.5g; Cholesterol 106mg; Calcium 104mg; Fibre 1.1g; Sodium 331mg.

LEMON MERINGUE PIE

CRISP SHORTCRUST IS FILLED WITH A MOUTHWATERING LEMON CREAM FILLING AND HEAPED WITH SOFT GOLDEN-TOPPED MERINGUE. THIS CLASSIC DESSERT NEVER FAILS TO PLEASE.

SERVES SIX

INGREDIENTS
3 large (US extra large) eggs,
  separated
150g/5oz/⅔ cup caster
  (superfine) sugar
grated rind and juice of 1 lemon
25g/1oz/½ cup fresh breadcrumbs
250ml/8fl oz/1 cup milk
For the pastry
115g/4oz/1 cup plain
  (all-purpose) flour
pinch of salt
50g/2oz/¼ cup butter, diced
50g/2oz/¼ cup lard (shortening) or
  white vegetable fat, diced
15ml/1 tbsp caster
  (superfine) sugar
15ml/1 tbsp chilled water

1 To make the pastry, sift the flour and salt into a mixing bowl. Rub or cut in the fats until the mixture resembles fine breadcrumbs. Stir in the caster sugar and enough chilled water to make a soft dough. Roll it out on a lightly floured surface and use to line a 21cm/8½in pie plate. Chill until required.

2 Meanwhile, place the egg yolks and 30ml/2 tbsp of the caster sugar in a bowl. Add the lemon rind and juice, the breadcrumbs and milk, mix lightly and leave to soak for 1 hour.

3 Preheat the oven to 200°C/400°F/ Gas 6. Beat the filling until smooth and pour into the chilled pastry case. Bake for 20 minutes, or until the filling has just set. Remove the pie from the oven and cool on a wire rack for 30 minutes or until a slight skin has formed on the surface. Lower the oven temperature to 180°C/350°F/Gas 4.

4 Whisk the egg whites until stiff peaks form. Gradually whisk in the remaining caster sugar to form a glossy meringue. Spoon on top of the filling and spread to the edge of the pastry, using the back of a spoon. Swirl the meringue slightly.

5 Bake the pie for 20–25 minutes, or until the meringue is crisp and golden brown. Allow to cool on a wire rack for 10 minutes before serving warm, or leave to cool completely and chill.

Energy 378Kcal/1586kJ; Protein 7.6g; Carbohydrate 46.3g, of which sugars 28.5g; Fat 19.5g, of which saturates 9.1g; Cholesterol 142mg; Calcium 114mg; Fibre 0.7g; Sodium 144mg.

KEY LIME PIE

THIS SPLENDID TART WITH ITS RICH LIME FILLING IS ONE OF AMERICA'S FAVOURITES. AS THE NAME SUGGESTS, IT ORIGINATED IN THE FLORIDA KEYS. FORGET ABOUT BEING BLUE, THINK SUN AND ENJOY!

SERVES TEN

INGREDIENTS
    4 eggs, separated
    400g/14oz can condensed milk
    grated rind and juice of 3 limes
    a few drops of green food
        colouring (optional)
    30ml/2 tbsp caster (superfine) sugar
    thinly pared lime rind and fresh mint
        leaves, to decorate
For the pastry
    225g/8oz/2 cups plain
        (all-purpose) flour
    115g/4oz/½ cup chilled butter, diced
    30ml/2 tbsp caster (superfine) sugar
    2 egg yolks
    pinch of salt
    30ml/2 tbsp chilled water
For the topping
    300ml/½ pint/1¼ cups double
        (heavy) cream
    2–3 limes, thinly sliced

1 To make the pastry, sift the flour into a mixing bowl, add the butter and rub in with your fingertips until the mixture resembles fine breadcrumbs. Add the sugar, egg yolks, salt and water, then mix to a soft dough.

2 Roll out the pastry on a lightly floured surface and use to line a deep 21cm/8½in fluted flan tin (tart pan), allowing the excess pastry to hang over the edge. Prick the pastry base with a fork and chill for at least 30 minutes.

3 Preheat the oven to 200°C/400°F/Gas 6. Trim off the excess pastry from around the edge of the pastry case (pie shell) using a sharp knife. If using a metal flan tin, you can just roll over the rim with a rolling pin. Line the pastry case with baking parchment or foil and baking beans.

4 Bake the pastry case blind for about 10 minutes. Remove the parchment or foil and beans and return the pastry case to the oven for 10 minutes more, until just cooked but not browned.

5 Meanwhile, beat the egg yolks in a large bowl until light and creamy, then beat in the condensed milk, with the lime rind and juice, until thoroughly combined. Add the food colouring, if using, and continue to beat until the mixture is thick.

6 In a grease-free bowl, whisk the egg whites to stiff peaks. Whisk in the caster sugar until the meringue is stiff, then fold into the lime mixture.

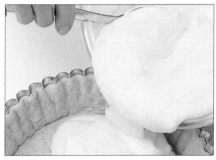

7 Lower the oven temperature to 160°C/325°F/Gas 3. Pour the lime filling into the pastry case, smoothing the top. Bake for 20–25 minutes until it has set and is turning brown. Cool, then chill.

8 Whip the cream for the topping and spoon it around the edge of the pie. Cut each lime slice from the centre to the edge, then twist it and arrange between the spoonfuls of cream. Decorate with lime rind and mint leaves.

Energy 508Kcal/2121kJ; Protein 9.1g; Carbohydrate 47.8g, of which sugars 30.6g; Fat 32.6g, of which saturates 19.3g; Cholesterol 171g; Calcium 182mg; Fibre 0.7g; Sodium 167mg.

CHOCOLATE MOUSSE CUPS

HEADY, AROMATIC ESPRESSO COFFEE ADDS A DISTINCTIVE FLAVOUR TO THIS SMOOTH, RICH MOUSSE.
SERVE IT IN STYLISH CHOCOLATE CUPS TO BRING A SENSE OF OCCASION TO THE DESSERT COURSE.

SERVES FOUR

INGREDIENTS
   225g/8oz plain (semisweet) chocolate
   45ml/3 tbsp brewed espresso
   25g/1oz/2 tbsp unsalted
    (sweet) butter
   4 eggs, separated
   mascarpone or clotted cream,
    to serve (optional)
   mint sprigs, to decorate (optional)
For the chocolate cups
   225g/8oz plain (semisweet) chocolate

1 For each chocolate cup, cut a double thickness 15cm/6in square of foil. Mould it around a small orange, leaving the edges and corners loose to make a cup shape. Remove the orange and press the base of the foil case (shell) gently on the work surface to make a flat base. Repeat to make four foil cups.

2 For the cups, break the chocolate into small pieces and place in a bowl set over very hot, but not boiling, water. Stir occasionally until the chocolate is smooth and has melted.

3 Spoon the chocolate into the foil cups, spreading it up the sides with the back of a spoon to give a ragged edge. Chill for 30 minutes or until set hard. Gently peel away the foil, starting at the top edge.

4 To make the chocolate mousse, put the plain chocolate and brewed espresso into a bowl set over a pan of hot water and melt as before. When smooth and liquid, add the unsalted butter, a little at a time. Remove the pan from the heat then stir in the egg yolks.

5 Whisk the egg whites in a bowl until stiff, but not dry, then fold into the chocolate mixture. Pour into a bowl and chill for at least 3 hours.

6 To serve, scoop the chilled mousse carefully into the chocolate cups. Add a scoop of mascarpone or clotted cream and decorate with a sprig of fresh mint, if using.

Energy 709Kcal/2963kJ; Protein 13.2g; Carbohydrate 71.5g, of which sugars 70.5g; Fat 43.3g, of which saturates 24g; Cholesterol 248g; Calcium 73mg; Fibre 2.8g; Sodium 129mg.

RASPBERRY MOUSSE GÂTEAU

A LAVISH QUANTITY OF RASPBERRIES GIVES THIS GÂTEAU ITS VIBRANT COLOUR AND FULL FLAVOUR. MAKE IT AT THE HEIGHT OF SUMMER, WHEN RASPBERRIES ARE PLENTIFUL.

SERVES EIGHT TO TEN

INGREDIENTS

2 eggs
50g/2oz/¼ cup caster (superfine) sugar
50g/2oz/½ cup plain (all-purpose) flour
30ml/2 tbsp unsweetened cocoa powder
600g/1lb 5oz/3½ cups raspberries
115g/4oz/1 cup icing (confectioners') sugar
60ml/4 tbsp whisky (optional)
300ml/½ pint/1¼ cups whipping cream
2 egg whites

1 Preheat the oven to 180°C/350°F/ Gas 4. Grease and line a 23cm/9in springform cake tin (pan). Whisk the eggs and sugar in a heatproof bowl set over a pan of gently simmering water until the whisk leaves a trail when lifted. Remove the bowl from the heat and continue to whisk the mixture for 2 minutes.

2 Sift the flour and cocoa powder over the mixture and fold it in with a large metal spoon. Spoon the mixture into the tin and spread it gently to the edges. Bake for 12–15 minutes until just firm.

3 Leave to cool, then remove the cake from the tin and place it on a wire rack. Wash and dry the tin.

4 Line the sides of the clean tin with a strip of greaseproof paper and carefully lower the cake back into it. Freeze until the raspberry filling is ready.

5 Set aside 200g/7oz/generous 1 cup of the raspberries. Put the remainder in a clean bowl, stir in the icing sugar, and process to a purée in a food processor or blender. Strain the purée into a bowl, then stir in the whisky, if using.

6 Whip the cream to form soft peaks. Whisk the egg whites until they are stiff. Using a large metal spoon, fold the cream, then the egg whites into the raspberry purée.

7 Spread half the raspberry mixture over the cake. Sprinkle with the reserved raspberries. Spread the remaining raspberry mixture on top and level the surface. Cover and freeze the gâteau overnight.

8 Transfer the gâteau to the refrigerator at least 1 hour before serving. Remove it from the tin, place on a serving plate and serve in slices.

Energy 301Kcal/1260kJ; Protein 5.7g; Carbohydrate 31.4g, of which sugars 26g; Fat 17.9g, of which saturates 10.5g; Cholesterol 96mg; Calcium 67mg; Fibre 2.5g; Sodium 86mg.

BAKED CARAMEL CUSTARD

CUSTARDS ARE CLASSIC NURSERY PUDDINGS: THIS IS A MORE SOPHISTICATED TAKE ON THESE SIMPLE, NOURISHING DESSERTS. KNOWN AS CRÈME CARAMEL IN FRANCE AND FLAN IN SPAIN, THIS CHILLED CUSTARD HAS A RICH CARAMEL FLAVOUR WHICH IS WONDERFUL WITH CREAM AND STRAWBERRIES.

SERVES SIX TO EIGHT

INGREDIENTS
    250g/9oz/1¼ cups granulated sugar
    1 vanilla pod (bean)
    425ml/15fl oz/1¾ cups double
        (heavy) cream
    5 large (US extra large) eggs,
        plus 2 extra yolks
    thick cream and fresh strawberries,
        to serve

1 Put 175g/6oz/generous ¾ cup of the sugar in a small heavy pan with just enough water to moisten the sugar. Bring to the boil over a high heat, swirling the pan until the sugar is dissolved completely. Boil for about 5 minutes, without stirring, until the syrup turns a dark caramel colour.

2 Working quickly, pour the caramel into a 1 litre/1¾ pint/4 cup soufflé dish. Holding the dish with oven gloves, carefully swirl the dish to coat the base and sides evenly with the hot caramel mixture. Work quickly as the caramel soon sets and becomes hard. Set the dish aside to cool.

3 Preheat the oven to 160ºC/325ºF/ Gas 3. With a small sharp knife, carefully split the vanilla pod lengthways and scrape the black seeds into a pan. Add the cream and bring just to the boil over a medium-high heat, stirring frequently. Remove the pan from the heat, cover and set aside for about 20 minutes to cool.

4 In a bowl, whisk the eggs and egg yolks with the remaining sugar for 2–3 minutes until smooth and creamy.

5 Whisk in the hot cream and carefully strain the mixture into the caramel-lined dish. Cover tightly with foil.

VARIATION
For a special occasion, make individual baked custards in ramekin dishes. Coat 6–8 ramekins with the caramel and divide the custard mixture among them. Bake, in a roasting pan of water, for 25–30 minutes or until set. Slice the strawberries and marinate them in a little sugar and a liqueur or dessert wine, such as Amaretto or Muscat wine.

6 Place the dish in a roasting pan and pour in just enough boiling water to come halfway up the side of the dish.

7 Bake the custard for 40–45 minutes until just set. To test whether the custard is set, insert a knife about 5cm/2in from the edge; if it comes out clean, the custard should be ready.

8 Remove the soufflé dish from the roasting pan and leave to cool for at least 30 minutes, then place in the refrigerator and chill overnight.

9 To turn out, carefully run a sharp knife around the edge of the dish to loosen the custard.

10 Cover the dish with a serving plate and, holding them together very tightly, invert the dish and plate, allowing the custard to drop down on to the plate.

11 Gently lift one edge of the dish, allowing the caramel to run down over the sides and on to the plate, then carefully lift off the dish. Serve with thick cream and fresh strawberries.

Energy 622Kcal/2587kJ; Protein 9.6g; Carbohydrate 44.8g, of which sugars 44.8g; Fat 46.4g, of which saturates 26g; Cholesterol 386mg; Calcium 98mg; Fibre 0g; Sodium 103mg.

SUMMER PUDDING

THIS IS ONE OF THOSE GLORIOUS DESSERTS THAT WORKS WONDERS AND MAKES YOU FEEL A MILLION DOLLARS. FIRST — AND FOREMOST WHEN LIFE IS A LITTLE GLUM — IT LOOKS AND TASTES IRRESISTIBLE. SECOND, IT IS PACKED FULL OF FRUIT GOODNESS — VITAMINS GALORE TO PROTECT AND RESTORE.

SERVES FOUR TO SIX

INGREDIENTS

   8 x 1cm/½in thick slices of day-old
     white bread, crusts removed
   800g/1¾lb/7 cups mixed berry fruit,
     such as strawberries, raspberries,
     blackcurrants, redcurrants and
     blueberries
   50g/2oz/¼ cup golden caster
     (superfine) sugar
   lightly whipped double (heavy) cream
     or crème fraîche, to serve

1 Trim a slice of bread to fit in the base of a 1.2 litre/2 pint/5 cup pudding basin, then trim another 5–6 slices to line the sides of the basin.

2 Place all the fruit in a pan with the sugar. Cook gently for 4–5 minutes until the juices begin to run. Do not add any water. Allow the mixture to cool slightly, then spoon the berries and enough of their juices to moisten into the bread-lined pudding basin. Save any leftover juice to serve with the pudding.

3 Fold over the excess bread, then cover the fruit with the remaining bread slices, trimming them to fit. Place a small plate or saucer directly on top of the pudding, fitting it inside the basin. Weight it with a 900g/2lb weight if you have one, or use a couple of full cans.

4 Leave the pudding in the refrigerator for at least 8 hours or overnight. To serve, run a knife between the pudding and the basin and turn it out on to a plate. Spoon any reserved juices over the top and serve with whipped cream or crème fraîche.

Energy 230Kcal/977kJ; Protein 6.2g; Carbohydrate 51.7g, of which sugars 26.5g; Fat 1.2g, of which saturates 0g; Cholesterol 0mg; Calcium 98mg; Fibre 3g; Sodium 294mg.

BRANDIED APPLE CHARLOTTE

LOOSELY BASED ON A TRADITIONAL APPLE CHARLOTTE, THIS ICED VERSION COMBINES BRANDY-STEEPED DRIED APPLE WITH A SPICY RICOTTA CREAM TO MAKE AN UNUSUAL AND INSPIRING DESSERT.

SERVES EIGHT TO TEN

INGREDIENTS
- 130g/4½oz/¾ cup dried apples
- 75ml/5 tbsp brandy
- 50g/2oz/¼ cup unsalted (sweet) butter
- 115g/4oz/½ cup light muscovado (brown) sugar
- 2.5ml/½ tsp mixed (apple-pie) spice
- 60ml/4 tbsp water
- 75g/3oz/½ cup sultanas (golden raisins)
- 300g/11oz Madeira cake, cut into 1cm/½in slices
- 250g/9oz/generous 1 cup ricotta cheese
- 30ml/2 tbsp lemon juice
- 150ml/¼ pint/⅔ cup double (heavy) or whipping cream
- icing (confectioners') sugar and fresh mint sprigs, to decorate

1 Roughly chop the dried apples, then transfer them to a clean bowl. Pour over the brandy and set aside for about 1 hour or until most of the brandy has been absorbed.

2 Melt the butter in a frying pan. Add the sugar and stir over a low heat for 1 minute. Add the mixed spice, water and soaked apples, with any remaining brandy. Heat until just simmering, reduce the heat slightly, if necessary, and then cook gently for about 5 minutes or until the apples are tender. Stir in the sultanas and leave to cool completely.

3 Use the Madeira cake slices to line the sides of a 20cm/8in square or 20cm/8in round springform or loose-based cake tin (pan). Place in the freezer while you make the filling.

4 Beat the ricotta in a bowl until it has softened, then stir in the apple mixture and lemon juice. Whip the cream in a separate bowl and fold it in. Spoon the mixture into the lined tin and level the surface. Cover and freeze overnight.

5 Transfer the charlotte to the refrigerator 1 hour before serving. Invert it on to a serving plate, dust with sugar, and decorate with mint sprigs.

COOK'S TIP
Line the tin with clear film (plastic wrap) before placing the cake in it if you are concerned that the dessert will not turn out easily when it is frozen.

Energy 446Kcal/1869kJ; Protein 6g; Carbohydrate 54.4g, of which sugars 46.2g; Fat 21.9g, of which saturates 13.3g; Cholesterol 49mg; Calcium 119mg; Fibre 2.1g; Sodium 222mg.

MISSISSIPPI MUD PIE

THIS IS THE ULTIMATE IN CHOCOLATE DESSERTS — A DEEP PASTRY CASE, FILLED WITH CHOCOLATE CUSTARD AND TOPPED WITH A FLUFFY RUM MOUSSE AND A SMOTHERING OF WHIPPED CREAM.

SERVES SIX TO EIGHT

INGREDIENTS
   3 eggs, separated
   20ml/4 tsp cornflour (cornstarch)
   75g/3oz/6 tbsp caster
      (superfine) sugar
   400ml/14fl oz/1⅔ cups milk
   150g/5oz plain (semisweet)
      chocolate, broken up
   5ml/1 tsp vanilla extract
   15ml/1 tbsp powdered gelatine
   45ml/3 tbsp water
   30ml/2 tbsp dark rum
   175g/6fl oz/¾ cup double (heavy)
      cream, whipped
   a few chocolate curls,
      to decorate
For the pastry
   250g/9oz/2¼ cups plain
      (all-purpose) flour
   150g/5oz/⅔ cup butter, diced
   2 egg yolks
   15–30ml/1–2 tbsp chilled water

1 To make the pastry, sift the flour into a bowl and rub or cut in the butter until the mixture resembles breadcrumbs. Stir in the egg yolks with just enough chilled water to make a soft dough.

2 Roll out on a lightly floured surface and use to line a deep 23cm/9in flan tin (tart pan). Chill for 30 minutes. Preheat the oven to 190°C/375°F/Gas 5. Prick the pastry all over with a fork, line with foil and baking beans, then bake blind for 10 minutes.

3 Remove the foil and beans, return the pie to the oven and bake for about 10 minutes more until the pastry is crisp and golden. Cool in the tin.

4 To make the custard filling, mix the egg yolks, cornflour and 30ml/2 tbsp of the sugar in a bowl. Heat the milk in a pan until almost boiling, then beat into the egg mixture.

5 Return the custard mixture to the cleaned pan and stir over a low heat until the custard has thickened and is smooth. Pour half the custard into a bowl.

6 Melt the chocolate in a heatproof bowl set over a pan of hot water, then add to the custard in the bowl. Add the vanilla extract and mix well. Spread in the pastry case, cover closely with some baking parchment to prevent a skin from forming, cool, then chill until set.

7 Sprinkle the gelatine over the water in a small bowl, leave until spongy, then place over a pan of simmering water until all the gelatine has dissolved. Stir into the remaining custard, along with the rum. Whisk the egg whites until stiff peaks form, whisk in the remaining sugar, then quickly fold into the custard before it sets.

8 Spoon the mixture over the chocolate custard. Chill until set, then remove the pie from the tin. Spread whipped cream over the top, decorate with chocolate curls and serve immediately.

Energy 827Kcal/3454kJ; Protein 13g; Carbohydrate 83.5g, of which sugars 33.1g; Fat 50.2g, of which saturates 29.2g; Cholesterol 280mg; Calcium 200mg; Fibre 1.9g; Sodium 246mg.

BOSTON BANOFFEE PIE

SIMPLY PRESS THIS WONDERFULLY BISCUITY PASTRY INTO THE TIN, RATHER THAN ROLLING IT OUT.
ADD THE FUDGE-TOFFEE FILLING AND SLICED BANANA TOPPING AND IT'LL PROVE IRRESISTIBLE.

SERVES SIX

INGREDIENTS
   115g/4oz/½ cup butter, diced
   200g/7oz can skimmed, sweetened
      condensed milk
   115g/4oz/½ cup soft brown sugar
   30ml/2 tbsp golden (light corn) syrup
   2 small bananas, sliced
   a little lemon juice
   whipped cream and 5ml/1 tsp
      grated plain (semisweet) chocolate,
      to decorate
For the pastry
   150g/5oz/1¼ cups plain
      (all-purpose) flour
   115g/4oz/½ cup butter, diced
   50g/2oz/¼ cup caster
      (superfine) sugar

1 Preheat the oven to 160°C/325°F/
Gas 3. In a food processor, process the
flour and diced butter until crumbed.
Stir in the caster sugar and mix to form
a soft, pliable dough.

2 Press into a 20cm/8in loose-based
flan tin (tart pan). Bake for 30 minutes.

3 To make the filling, place the butter
in a pan with the condensed milk,
brown sugar and syrup. Heat gently,
stirring, until the butter has melted and
the sugar has completely dissolved.

4 Bring to a gentle boil and cook for
7–10 minutes, stirring constantly, until
the mixture thickens and turns a light
caramel colour.

5 Pour the hot caramel filling into the
pastry case and leave until completely
cold. Sprinkle the banana slices with
lemon juice to prevent them from
discolouring and arrange them in
overlapping circles on top of the filling,
leaving a gap in the centre. Pipe a
generous swirl of whipped cream in the
centre and sprinkle with the grated
chocolate. Serve immediately.

Energy 608Kcal/2547kJ; Protein 6.4g; Carbohydrate 78.5g, of which sugars 58.9g; Fat 32g, of which saturates 20.1g; Cholesterol 82mg; Calcium 169mg; Fibre 1.1g; Sodium 299mg.

Hot Puddings, Desserts and Drinks

Look no further than here for classic comforters.
Here are the nursery puddings, the fruit crumbles
and pies and the bedtime drinks that encouraged
happy childhood dreams.

CRÊPES WITH ORANGE SAUCE

CRÊPE-MAKING CAN BE VERY RELAXING ONCE THE FIRST COUPLE OF REJECTS ARE OUT OF THE WAY AND THE PAN TEMPERATURE IS JUST RIGHT. THIS IS ONE OF THE BEST WAYS TO ENJOY THIN CRÊPES.

SERVES SIX

INGREDIENTS
    115g/4oz/1 cup plain
        (all-purpose) flour
    1.5ml/¼ tsp salt
    25g/1oz/2 tbsp caster
        (superfine) sugar
    2 eggs, lightly beaten
    about 250ml/8fl oz/1 cup milk
    about 60ml/4 tbsp water
    30ml/2 tbsp orange flower water,
        Cointreau or other orange liqueur
    25g/1oz/2 tbsp unsalted (sweet)
        butter, melted, plus extra for frying
For the sauce
    75g/3oz/6 tbsp unsalted
        (sweet) butter
    50g/2oz/¼ cup caster
        (superfine) sugar
    grated rind and juice of
        1 large orange
    grated rind and juice of 1 lemon
    150ml/¼ pint/⅔ cup freshly
        squeezed orange juice
    60ml/4 tbsp Cointreau or other
        orange liqueur, plus more for
        flaming (optional)
    brandy, for flaming (optional)
    orange segments, to decorate

1 Sift the flour, salt and sugar into a large bowl. Make a well in the centre and pour in the eggs. Beat the eggs, gradually incorporating the flour.

2 Whisk in the milk, water and orange flower water or liqueur to make a very smooth batter. Strain into a jug (pitcher) and set aside for 20–30 minutes.

3 Heat an 18–20cm/7–8in crêpe pan (preferably non-stick) over a medium heat. If the crêpe batter has thickened, add a little more water or milk to thin it. Stir the melted butter into the batter.

4 Brush the hot pan with a little extra melted butter and pour in about 30ml/ 2 tbsp of batter. Quickly tilt and rotate the pan to cover the base evenly with a thin layer of batter. Cook for about 1 minute, or until the top is set and the base is golden. With a metal spatula, lift the edge to check the colour, then carefully turn over the crêpe and cook for 20–30 seconds, just to set. Tip out on to a plate.

5 Continue cooking the crêpes, stirring the batter occasionally and brushing the pan with a little more melted butter as and when necessary. Place a sheet of clear film (plastic wrap) or baking parchment between each crêpe as they are stacked to prevent them from sticking. (The crêpes can be prepared ahead to this point – put them in a plastic bag and chill until ready to use.)

6 To make the sauce, melt the butter in a large frying pan over a medium-low heat, then stir in the sugar, orange and lemon rind and juice, the additional orange juice and the orange liqueur.

7 Place a crêpe in the pan browned-side down, swirling gently to coat with the sauce. Fold it in half, then in half again to form a triangle, and push to the side of the pan. Continue heating and folding the crêpes until all are warm and covered with the sauce.

8 To flame the crêpes, heat 30–45ml/ 2–3 tbsp each of orange liqueur and brandy in a small pan over a medium heat. Remove the pan from the heat, carefully ignite the liquid with a match then pour evenly over the crêpes. Sprinkle over the orange segments and serve immediately.

COOK'S TIP
Cointreau is the world's leading brand of orange liqueur. It is colourless and flavoured with a mixture of bitter orange peel and sweet oranges.

DEEP-DISH APPLE PIE

THIS IS PIE LIKE MOTHER USED TO MAKE, WITH MELT-IN-THE-MOUTH SHORTCRUST PASTRY. INSIDE, SUGAR, SPICES AND FLOUR CREATE A DELICIOUSLY THICK AND SYRUPY SAUCE WITH THE APPLE JUICES.

4 Put a baking sheet in the oven and preheat to 200°C/400°F/Gas 6. Roll out just over half the pastry and use to line a 23cm/9in pie dish that is 4cm/1½in deep, allowing the pastry to overhang the edges slightly. Spoon in the filling, doming the apple slices in the centre.

5 Roll out the remaining pastry to form the lid. Lightly brush the edges of the pastry case with a little water, then place the lid over the apple filling.

6 Trim the pastry with a sharp knife. Gently press the edges together to seal, then knock up the edge. Re-roll the pastry trimmings and cut out apple and leaf shapes. Brush the top of the pie with egg white. Arrange the pastry apples and leaves on top.

7 Brush again with egg white, then sprinkle with golden granulated sugar. Make two small slits in the top of the pie to allow steam to escape.

8 Bake for 30 minutes, then lower the oven temperature to 180°C/350°F/Gas 4 and bake for a further 15 minutes until the pastry is golden and the apples are soft – check by inserting a small sharp knife or skewer through one of the slits in the top of the pie. Serve hot, with whipped cream.

SERVES SIX

INGREDIENTS
  115g/4oz/½ cup caster
    (superfine) sugar
  45ml/3 tbsp plain (all-purpose) flour
  2.5ml/½ tsp ground cinnamon
  finely grated rind of 1 orange
  900g/2lb cooking apples
  1 egg white, lightly beaten
  30ml/2 tbsp golden granulated sugar
  whipped cream, to serve
For the pastry
  350g/12oz/3 cups plain
    (all-purpose) flour
  pinch of salt
  175g/6oz/¾ cup butter, diced
  about 75ml/5 tbsp chilled water

1 To make the pastry, sift the flour and salt into a mixing bowl and rub or cut in the butter until the mixture resembles fine breadcrumbs.

2 Sprinkle over the water and mix to a firm, soft dough. Knead lightly for a few seconds until smooth. Wrap in clear film (plastic wrap) and chill for 30 minutes.

3 Combine the caster sugar, flour, cinnamon and orange rind in a bowl. Peel, core and thinly slice the apples. Add to the sugar mixture in the bowl, then toss gently with your fingertips until they are all evenly coated.

Energy 600Kcal/2524kJ; Protein 7.7g; Carbohydrate 91.9g, of which sugars 39.8g; Fat 25g, of which saturates 15.3g; Cholesterol 62mg; Calcium 120mg; Fibre 4.5g; Sodium 193mg.

SPICED APPLE CRUMBLE

ANY FRUIT CAN BE USED IN THIS POPULAR PUD, BUT AUTUMNAL BLACKBERRY AND APPLE ARE A REASSURINGLY FAMILIAR DUO. HAZELNUT AND CARDAMOM BRING CRUNCH AND ZING TO THE TOPPING.

SERVES FOUR TO SIX

INGREDIENTS
  butter, for greasing
  450g/1lb cooking apples
  115g/4oz/1 cup blackberries
  grated rind and juice of 1 orange
  50g/2oz/⅓ cup light muscovado
    (brown) sugar
  custard, to serve
For the topping
  175g/6oz/1½ cups plain (all-purpose)
    flour
  75g/3oz/⅓ cup butter
  75g/3oz/⅓ cup caster sugar
  25g/1oz/¼ cup chopped hazelnuts
  2.5ml/½ tsp crushed cardamom
    seeds

1 Preheat the oven to 200°C/400°F/ Gas 6. Generously butter a 1.2 litre/ 2 pint/5 cup baking dish. Peel and core the apples, then slice them into the prepared baking dish. Level the surface, then scatter the blackberries over. Sprinkle the orange rind and light muscovado sugar evenly over the top, then pour over the orange juice. Set the fruit mixture aside while you make the crumble topping.

2 Make the topping. Sift the flour into a bowl and rub in the butter until the mixture resembles coarse breadcrumbs. Stir in the caster sugar, hazelnuts and cardamom seeds. Scatter the topping over the top of the fruit.

3 Press the topping around the edges of the dish to seal in the juices. Bake for 30–35 minutes or until the crumble is golden. Serve hot, with custard.

Energy 504Kcal/2120kJ; Protein 5.9g; Carbohydrate 79.7g, of which sugars 46.3g; Fat 20.1g, of which saturates 10.2g; Cholesterol 40g; Calcium 108mg; Fibre 4.5g; Sodium 121mg.

BLACKBERRY CHARLOTTE

THE PERFECT WARMER FOR COLD DAYS, SERVE THIS CHARLOTTE WITH WHIPPED CREAM OR HOME-MADE CUSTARD.

SERVES FOUR

INGREDIENTS
   65g/2½oz/5 tbsp unsalted (sweet)
      butter
   175g/6oz/3 cups fresh white
      breadcrumbs
   50g/2oz/4 tbsp soft brown sugar
   60ml/4 tbsp golden (light corn) syrup
   finely grated rind and juice of
      2 lemons
   50g/2oz walnut halves
   450g/1lb blackberries
   450g/1lb cooking apples, peeled,
      cored and finely sliced

3 Process the walnuts until they are finely ground.

4 Arrange a thin layer of blackberries on the dish. Top with a thin layer of crumbs.

5 Add a thin layer of apple, topping it with another thin layer of crumbs.

6 Repeat the process with another layer of blackberries, followed by a layer of crumbs. Continue until you have used up all the ingredients, finishing with a layer of crumbs. The mixture should be piled well above the top edge of the dish, because it shrinks during cooking. Bake for 30 minutes, until the crumbs are golden and the fruit is soft.

1 Preheat the oven to 180°C/350°F/ Gas 4. Grease a 450ml/¾ pint/2 cup dish with 15g/½oz/1 tbsp of the butter. Melt the remaining butter and add the breadcrumbs. Sauté them for 5–7 minutes, until the crumbs are a little crisp and golden. Leave to cool slightly.

2 Place the sugar, syrup, lemon rind and juice in a small pan and gently warm them. Add the crumbs.

Energy 546Kcal/2294kJ; Protein 8.5g; Carbohydrate 81g, of which sugars 48.2g; Fat 23.1g, of which saturates 9.2g; Cholesterol 35mg; Calcium 133mg; Fibre 6.7g; Sodium 498mg.

FRESH CURRANT BREAD AND BUTTER PUDDING

FRESH MIXED CURRANTS BRING A WIDE~AWAKE CHARACTER TO THIS SCRUMPTIOUS HOT PUDDING.

SERVES SIX

INGREDIENTS

  8 medium-thick slices day-old bread,
    crusts removed
  50g/2oz/¼ cup butter, softened
  115g/4oz/1 cup redcurrants
  115g/4oz/1 cup blackcurrants
  4 eggs, beaten
  75g/3oz/6 tbsp caster (superfine)
    sugar
  475ml/16fl oz/2 cups creamy
    milk
  5ml/1 tsp vanilla extract
  freshly grated nutmeg
  30ml/2 tbsp demerara sugar
  single (light) cream, to serve

1 Preheat the oven to 160°C/325°F/
Gas 3. Generously butter a 1.2 litre/
2 pint/5 cup oval baking dish.

2 Spread the slices of bread generously
with the butter, then cut them in half
diagonally. Layer the slices in the dish,
buttered side up, scattering the currants
between the layers.

3 Beat the eggs and caster sugar
lightly together in a large mixing bowl,
then gradually whisk in the milk, vanilla
extract and a large pinch of freshly
grated nutmeg.

4 Pour the milk mixture over the bread,
pushing the slices down. Scatter the
demerara sugar and a little nutmeg over
the top. Place the dish in a baking tin
and fill with hot water to come halfway
up the sides of the dish. Bake for
40 minutes, then increase the oven
temperature to 180°C/350°F/Gas 4 and
bake for 20–25 minutes more or until
the top is golden. Cool slightly, then
serve with single cream.

Energy 335Kcal/1406kJ; Protein 11.2g; Carbohydrate 41.3g, of which sugars 24.5g; Fat 15.1g, of which saturates 7.6g; Cholesterol 181mg; Calcium 180mg; Fibre 1.9g; Sodium 330mg.

BREAD AND BUTTER PUDDING WITH WHISKEY SAUCE

THIS IS COMFORT FOOD AT ITS VERY BEST. THE WHISKEY SAUCE IS HEAVENLY, BUT IF YOU ARE NOT KEEN ON THE ALCOHOL, THE PUDDING CAN ALSO BE SERVED WITH CHILLED CREAM OR VANILLA ICE CREAM — THE CONTRAST BETWEEN THE HOT AND COLD IS DELICIOUS.

SERVES SIX

INGREDIENTS

   8 slices white bread, buttered
   115g/4oz/⅔ cup sultanas (golden
     raisins), or mixed dried fruit
   2.5ml/½ tsp grated nutmeg
   150g/5oz/¾ cup caster (superfine)
     sugar
   2 large (US extra large) eggs
   300ml/½ pint/1¼ cups single
     (light) cream
   450ml/¾ pint/scant 2 cups milk
   5ml/1 tsp vanilla extract
   light muscovado (brown) sugar, for
     sprinkling (optional)
For the whiskey sauce
   150g/5oz/10 tbsp butter
   115g/4oz/generous ½ cup caster
     (superfine) sugar
   1 egg
   45ml/3 tbsp Irish whiskey

1 Preheat the oven to 180°C/350°F/ Gas 4. Remove the crusts from the bread and put four slices, buttered side down, in the base of an ovenproof dish. Sprinkle with the fruit, some of the nutmeg and 15ml/1 tbsp of the sugar.

2 Place the remaining four slices of bread on top, buttered side down, and sprinkle again with nutmeg and 15ml/1 tbsp of the sugar.

3 Beat the eggs lightly, add the cream, milk, vanilla extract and the remaining sugar, and mix well to make a custard. Pour this mixture over the bread, and sprinkle light muscovado sugar over the top, if you like to have a crispy crust. Bake in the preheated oven for 1 hour, or until all the liquid has been absorbed and the pudding is risen and brown.

4 Meanwhile, make the whiskey sauce: melt the butter in a heavy pan, add the caster sugar and dissolve over gentle heat. Remove from the heat and add the egg, whisking vigorously, and then add the whiskey. Serve the pudding on hot serving plates, with the whiskey sauce poured over the top.

Energy 757Kcal/3168kJ; Protein 11.7g; Carbohydrate 82g, of which sugars 65.2g; Fat 40.8g, of which saturates 24.3g; Cholesterol 207mg; Calcium 232mg; Fibre 0.9g; Sodium 472mg

SPICED PEARS WITH NUT CRUMBLE

AN ALL-TIME FAVOURITE, THIS CRUMBLE HAS A CRUNCHY PECAN NUT AND OAT TOPPING, WHICH COMPLEMENTS THE SPICY PEARS HIDDEN BENEATH.

SERVES FOUR TO SIX

INGREDIENTS
900g/2lb pears
30ml/2 tbsp lemon juice
40g/1½oz/3 tbsp caster (superfine)
   sugar
5ml/1 tsp mixed (apple pie) spice
2.5ml/½ tsp grated nutmeg
vanilla ice cream, to serve
For the crumble topping
75g/3oz/⅔ cup plain (all-purpose)
   flour
75g/3oz/6 tbsp butter
50g/2oz/¼ cup light muscovado
   (brown) sugar
50g/2oz/½ cup pecan nuts or
   walnuts, chopped
40g/1½oz/scant ½ cup
   rolled oats

1 Peel the pears if you like, then halve them and remove the cores. Cut each pear into six wedges and toss in the lemon juice.

2 Place the pears in an ovenproof dish, add the sugar, mixed spice and nutmeg and mix together. Cover with a lid or foil, place in an unheated oven, set the oven to 200°C/400°F/Gas 6 and cook for 25 minutes.

3 Meanwhile, prepare the crumble topping. Sift the flour into a bowl and rub in the butter, then stir in the sugar, nuts and rolled oats.

4 Uncover the dish and stir gently to rearrange the fruit. Spoon the crumble mixture over the pears, then return to the oven for 25–30 minutes, or until the crumble is golden. Serve warm, with vanilla ice cream.

Energy 365Kcal/1523kJ; Protein 3.5g; Carbohydrate 42.9g, of which sugars 33.2g; Fat 21g, of which saturates 7.4g; Cholesterol 27mg; Calcium 57mg; Fibre 4.3g; Sodium 82mg.

APRICOT PANETTONE PUDDING

PANETTONE AND PECAN NUTS MAKE A RICH ADDITION TO THIS "NO-BUTTER" VERSION OF A TRADITIONAL BREAD AND BUTTER PUDDING.

SERVES SIX

INGREDIENTS

sunflower oil, for greasing
350g/12oz panettone, sliced into
   triangles
25g/1oz/¼ cup pecan nuts
75g/3oz/⅓ cup ready-to-eat dried
   apricots, chopped
500ml/17fl oz/generous 2 cups
   full-cream (whole) milk
5ml/1 tsp vanilla extract
1 large (US extra large) egg, beaten
30ml/2 tbsp maple syrup
freshly grated nutmeg
demerara (raw) sugar, for sprinkling

1 Lightly grease a 1 litre/1¾ pint/4 cup ovenproof dish. Arrange half of the panettone triangles in the dish, sprinkle over half the pecan nuts and all of the chopped, dried apricots, then add another layer of panettone on top.

COOK'S TIP
Panettone is a light fruit cake originally from northern Italy but now popular all over the world. It is traditionally eaten at festivals such as Christmas or Easter. Panettone is baked in cylindrical moulds, giving it a distinctive shape. You can now find panettone in different flavours – the coffee-flavoured type is particularly good.

2 Heat the milk and vanilla extract in a small pan until the milk just simmers. Put the egg and maple syrup in a large bowl, grate in about 2.5ml/½ tsp nutmeg, then whisk in the hot milk.

3 Preheat the oven to 200°C/400°F/ Gas 6. Pour the egg mixture over the panettone, lightly pressing down the bread so that it is submerged. Leave the pudding to stand for about 10 minutes, to allow the panettone slices to soak up a little of the liquid.

4 Sprinkle over the reserved pecan nuts and sprinkle a little demerara sugar and freshly grated nutmeg over the top. Bake for 40–45 minutes until the pudding is risen and golden brown. Serve hot.

Energy 294Kcal/1237kJ; Protein 9.4g; Carbohydrate 43.2g, of which sugars 21.8g; Fat 10.4g, of which saturates 3.7g; Cholesterol 44mg; Calcium 180mg; Fibre 2.3g; Sodium 248mg.

PEAR, ALMOND AND GROUND RICE PIE

GROUND RICE GIVES A DISTINCTIVE, SLIGHTLY GRAINY TEXTURE TO PUDDINGS THAT GOES PARTICULARLY WELL WITH AUTUMN FRUIT. PEARS AND ALMONDS ARE A DIVINE COMBINATION.

2 Place the butter and caster sugar in a mixing bowl and beat together using a wooden spoon or electric mixer until light and fluffy, then beat in the eggs, one at a time, and the almond extract. Fold in the flour and the ground rice.

3 Carefully spoon the creamed mixture over the quartered pears in the flan or pie dish and then level the surface with a palette knife or metal spatula.

4 Sprinkle the flaked almonds evenly over the top of the creamed mixture, then bake the flan for about 30 minutes, or until the topping springs back when touched lightly and is a golden brown colour. Serve warm or cold with custard or crème fraîche.

SERVES SIX

INGREDIENTS
 4 ripe pears
 25g/1oz/2 tbsp soft light brown sugar
 115g/4oz/½ cup unsalted (sweet) butter,
   at room temperature
 115g/4oz/generous ½ cup caster
   (superfine) sugar
 2 eggs
 a few drops of almond extract
 75g/3oz/⅔ cup self-raising
   (self-rising) flour
 50g/2oz/⅓ cup ground rice
 25g/1oz/¼ cup flaked (sliced) almonds
 pouring custard or crème fraîche,
   to serve

1 Preheat the oven to 180°C/350°F/ Gas 4. Grease a shallow 25cm/10in flan or pie dish, then peel and quarter the pears and arrange them in the dish. Sprinkle with the brown sugar.

Energy 396Kcal/1656kJ; Protein 5.2g; Carbohydrate 50.9g, of which sugars 34.8g; Fat 20.2g, of which saturates 10.7g; Cholesterol 104mg; Calcium 92mg; Fibre 2.9g; Sodium 190mg.

PLUM CHARLOTTES WITH FOAMY KIRSCH SAUCE

THESE INDIVIDUAL PUDDINGS, COOKED IN MINI EARTHENWARE DISHES, CONCEAL A FRESH PLUM
FILLING AND ARE SERVED ON A POOL OF LIGHT, FROTHY KIRSCH-FLAVOURED SAUCE.

SERVES FOUR

INGREDIENTS
115g/4oz/½ cup butter, melted
50g/2oz/4 tbsp demerara (raw) sugar
450g/1lb ripe plums, stoned (pitted)
   and thickly sliced
25g/1oz/2 tbsp caster (superfine) sugar
30ml/2 tbsp water
1.5ml/¼ tsp ground cinnamon
25g/1oz/¼ cup ground almonds
8–10 large slices of white bread
For the Kirsch sauce
3 egg yolks
40g/1½oz/3 tbsp caster (superfine)
   sugar
30ml/2 tbsp Kirsch

2 Place the stoned plum slices in a pan with the caster sugar, water and ground cinnamon and cook gently for 5 minutes, or until the plums have softened slightly. Leave them to cool, then stir in the ground almonds.

5 Divide the plum mixture among the lined dishes. Place the bread rounds on top and brush with the remaining butter. Place the ramekins on a baking sheet and bake for 25 minutes.

1 Preheat the oven to 190°C/375°F/ Gas 5. Line the base of four individual 10cm/4in-diameter deep, earthenware ramekin dishes with baking parchment. Brush evenly and thoroughly with a little of the melted butter, then sprinkle each dish with a little of the demerara sugar, rotating the dish in your hands to coat each dish evenly.

3 Cut the crusts off the bread and then use a plain pastry cutter to cut out four rounds to fit the bases of the ramekins. Dip the bread rounds into the melted butter and fit them into the dishes. Cut four more rounds to fit the tops of the dishes and set aside.

4 Cut the remaining bread into strips, dip into the melted butter and use to line the sides of the ramekins completely.

6 Just before the charlottes are ready place the egg yolks and caster sugar for the sauce in a bowl. Whisk together until pale. Place the bowl over a pan of simmering water and whisk in the Kirsch. Continue whisking until the mixture is very light and frothy.

7 Remove the charlottes from the oven and turn out on to warm serving plates. Pour a little sauce over and around the charlottes and serve immediately.

COOK'S TIP
For an extra indulgent dessert, serve the puddings with lightly whipped double (heavy) cream flavoured with extra Kirsch and sweetened to taste with a little sifted icing (confectioners') sugar.

VARIATIONS
• Slices of peeled pear or eating apples can be used in this recipe instead of the stoned, sliced plums.
• If using apples or pears replace the Kirsch in the foamy sauce with Calvados or another apple brandy.

Energy 600Kcal/2513kJ; Protein 9.1g; Carbohydrate 69.6g, of which sugars 44.2g; Fat 32.5g, of which saturates 16.5g; Cholesterol 218mg; Calcium 128mg; Fibre 3.1g; Sodium 467mg.

BAKED MAPLE AND PECAN CROISSANT PUDDING

THIS VARIATION OF THE CLASSIC ENGLISH BREAD AND BUTTER PUDDING USES CROISSANTS, WHICH GIVE A LIGHT FLUFFY TEXTURE. PECANS, BRANDY-LACED SULTANAS AND MAPLE SYRUP-FLAVOURED CUSTARD COMPLETE THIS MOUTHWATERING DESSERT.

SERVES FOUR

INGREDIENTS

  75g/3oz/generous ½ cup sultanas
    (golden raisins)
  45ml/3 tbsp brandy
  50g/2oz/¼ cup butter, plus extra
    for greasing
  4 large croissants
  40g/1½oz/⅓ cup pecan nuts,
    roughly chopped
  3 eggs, lightly beaten
  300ml/½ pint/1¼ cups milk
  150ml/¼ pint/⅔ cup single (light)
    cream
  120ml/4fl oz/½ cup maple syrup
  25g/1oz/2 tbsp demerara (raw) sugar
  maple syrup and pouring (half-and-
    half) cream, to serve (optional)

1 Place the sultanas and brandy in a small pan and heat gently, until warm. Leave to stand for 1 hour. Lightly grease the base and sides of a wide, shallow ovenproof dish.

2 Cut the croissants (see Cook's Tip) into thick slices, then spread with butter on one side.

3 Arrange the croissant slices, butter-side uppermost and slightly overlapping, in the greased dish. Sprinkle the brandy-soaked sultanas and the roughly chopped pecan nuts over the buttered croissant slices.

4 In a large bowl, beat the eggs and milk together, then gradually beat in the single cream and maple syrup.

5 Pour the egg custard through a sieve (strainer), over the croissants, fruit and nuts in the dish. Leave the uncooked pudding to stand for 30 minutes, so that some of the egg custard liquid is absorbed by the croissants.

6 Sprinkle the demerara sugar evenly over the top, then cover the dish and place in an unheated oven. Set the oven to 180°C/350°F/Gas 4 and bake for 40 minutes. Remove the lid and continue to cook for about 20 minutes, or until the custard is set and the top is golden.

7 Leave the pudding to cool for about 15 minutes before serving warm with extra maple syrup and a little pouring cream, if you like.

COOK'S TIPS
• This dessert is perfect for using up leftover croissants. Slightly stale one-day-old croissants are easier to slice and butter; they also soak up the custard more easily. Thickly sliced one-day-old bread or large slices of brioche could be used instead.
• Pecan nuts are an elongated nut in a glossy red oval-shaped shell, but are usually sold shelled. They are native to the USA and have a sweet, mild flavour. Pecans are most commonly used in pecan pie but are also popular in ice creams and cakes. Walnuts can be substituted for pecans in most recipes, and they would be perfect in this one if you don't have any pecan nuts.

Energy 731Kcal/3056kJ; Protein 15g; Carbohydrate 72.3g, of which sugars 49.4g; Fat 45.6g, of which saturates 19.5g; Cholesterol 226mg; Calcium 217mg; Fibre 1.8g; Sodium 507mg.

COCONUT RICE PUDDING

A DELICIOUS ADAPTATION OF THE CLASSIC CREAMY RICE PUDDING, THIS DESSERT IS FLAVOURED WITH COCONUT MILK AND FINISHED WITH A COCONUT CRUST.

SERVES FOUR

INGREDIENTS

   75g/3oz/scant ½ cup short grain
     pudding rice
   40g/1½oz/3 tbsp caster
     (superfine) sugar
   2.5ml/½ tsp vanilla extract
   300ml/½ pint/1¼ cups milk
   400ml/14fl oz/1⅔ cups coconut milk
   105ml/7 tbsp single (light) cream
   30ml/2 tbsp desiccated (dry
     unsweetened shredded) coconut or
     slivers of fresh coconut

1 Lightly grease an ovenproof dish, and place in it the rice, sugar, vanilla extract, milk, coconut milk and cream.

2 Cover with a lid or foil and place in a cold oven. Set the oven to 180°C/350°F/ Gas 4 and cook for 1 hour.

3 Uncover the dish, stir the pudding gently, then re-cover and cook for a further 30–45 minutes, or until the rice is tender.

4 Uncover, stir again, then sprinkle with desiccated or fresh coconut and bake uncovered for 10–15 minutes, until brown.

Energy 259Kcal/1087kJ; Protein 5.8g; Carbohydrate 34g, of which sugars 19.9g; Fat 11.6g, of which saturates 8.2g; Cholesterol 19mg; Calcium 153mg; Fibre 1g; Sodium 153mg.

CITRUS AND CARAMEL CUSTARDS

THESE SPANISH-STYLE CUSTARDS, MADE RICH WITH CREAM AND EGG YOLKS, ARE DELICATELY SCENTED WITH TANGY CITRUS FLAVOURS AND AROMATIC CINNAMON.

SERVES FOUR

INGREDIENTS
  450ml/¾ pint/scant 2 cups milk
  150ml/¼ pint/⅔ cup single
    (light) cream
  1 cinnamon stick, broken in half
  thinly pared rind of ½ lemon
  thinly pared rind of ½ orange
  4 egg yolks
  5ml/1 tsp cornflour (cornstarch)
  40g/1½oz/3 tbsp caster (superfine)
    sugar
  grated rind of ½ lemon
  grated rind of ½ orange
  icing (confectioners') sugar,
    for sprinkling

1 Place the milk and cream in a pan. Add the cinnamon stick and the strips of pared citrus rind. Bring to the boil, then simmer for 10 minutes.

2 Preheat the oven to 160°C/325°F/ Gas 3. Whisk the egg yolks, cornflour and caster sugar together. Remove the rinds and cinnamon from the hot milk and cream and discard. Whisk the hot milk and cream into the egg yolk mixture.

3 Stir the grated citrus rind into the custard mixture. Pour into four individual cazuelas, each about 13cm/5in in diameter. Place in a roasting pan and pour warm water into the pan to reach three-quarters of the way up the sides. Bake for 25–30 minutes, or until the custards are just set. Remove the dishes from the water; leave to cool, then chill.

4 Preheat the grill (broiler) to high. Sprinkle the custards liberally with icing sugar and place under the grill until the tops turn golden brown and caramelize.

COOK'S TIPS
• Prepare the grated rind first, then cut a few strips of rind from the ungrated side of the citrus fruits using a swivel-bladed vegetable peeler.
• You can use a special cook's gas-gun or salamander to caramelize the tops instead of grilling (broiling) them.

Energy 225Kcal/939kJ; Protein 8g; Carbohydrate 16.6g, of which sugars 16.6g; Fat 14.6g, of which saturates 7.3g; Cholesterol 229mg; Calcium 197mg; Fibre 0g; Sodium 69mg.

CHOCOLATE PUDDING <u>WITH</u> RUM CUSTARD

WITH MELTING MOMENTS OF CHOCOLATE IN EVERY MOUTHFUL, THESE LITTLE PUDDINGS WON'T LAST LONG. THE RUM CUSTARD TURNS THEM INTO A MORE ADULT PUDDING; FOR A FAMILY DESSERT, FLAVOUR THE CUSTARD WITH VANILLA OR ORANGE RIND INSTEAD.

SERVES SIX

INGREDIENTS
   115g/4oz/½ cup butter, plus extra
     for greasing
   115g/4oz/½ cup soft light brown sugar
   2 eggs, beaten
   a few drops of vanilla extract
   45ml/3 tbsp unsweetened cocoa
     powder
   115g/4oz/1 cup self-raising
     (self-rising) flour
   75g/3oz bitter (semisweet) chocolate,
     chopped
   a little milk, warmed
For the rum custard
   250ml/8fl oz/1 cup milk
   15ml/1 tbsp caster (superfine) sugar
   2 egg yolks
   10ml/2 tsp cornflour (cornstarch)
   30ml/2 tbsp rum

1 Lightly grease a 1.2 litre/2 pint/5 cup heatproof bowl or six individual dariole moulds. Cream the butter and sugar until pale and creamy. Gently blend in the eggs and the vanilla extract.

2 Sift together the cocoa and flour, and fold gently into the egg mixture with the chopped chocolate and sufficient milk to give a soft dropping consistency.

3 Spoon the mixture into the bowl or moulds, cover with buttered baking parchment and tie down. Fill a pan with 2.5–5cm/1–2in water, place the puddings in the pan, cover with a lid and bring to the boil. Steam the large pudding for 1½–2 hours and the individual puddings for 45–50 minutes, topping up with water if necessary. When firm, turn out on to warm plates.

4 To make the rum custard, bring the milk and sugar to the boil. Whisk together the egg yolks and cornflour, then pour on the hot milk, whisking constantly. Return the mixture to the pan and stir continuously while it slowly comes back to the boil. Allow the sauce to simmer gently as it thickens, stirring all the time. Remove from the heat and stir in the rum.

COOK'S TIP
To microwave, spoon the mixture into a microwave-proof basin (at least 300ml/½ pint/1¼ cups larger than necessary). Cover loosely with clear film (plastic wrap) and microwave on full power for 5 minutes. Leave to stand for 5 minutes.

Energy 458Kcal/1915kJ; Protein 8.3g; Carbohydrate 49g, of which sugars 31.5g; Fat 25.6g, of which saturates 14.5g; Cholesterol 186mg; Calcium 145mg; Fibre 1.8g; Sodium 302mg.

STICKY COFFEE AND GINGER PUDDING

THIS COFFEE-CAPPED FEATHER-LIGHT SPONGE IS MADE WITH BREADCRUMBS AND GROUND ALMONDS.
SERVE WITH CREAMY CUSTARD OR SCOOPS OF VANILLA ICE CREAM FOR GROWN-UP NURSERY PUDDING.

SERVES FOUR

INGREDIENTS
- 30ml/2 tbsp soft light brown sugar
- 25g/1oz/2 tbsp preserved stem ginger, chopped, plus 75ml/5 tbsp ginger syrup
- 30ml/2 tbsp mild-flavoured ground coffee
- 115g/4oz/generous ½ cup caster (superfine) sugar
- 3 eggs, separated
- 25g/1oz/¼ cup plain (all-purpose) flour
- 5ml/1 tsp ground ginger
- 65g/2½oz/generous 1 cup fresh white breadcrumbs
- 25g/1oz/¼ cup ground almonds

1 Preheat the oven to 180°C/350°F/Gas 4. Grease and line the base of a 750ml/1¼ pint/3 cup ovenproof bowl, then sprinkle in the sugar and chopped stem ginger.

2 Put the ground coffee in a small bowl. Heat the ginger syrup until almost boiling; pour into the coffee. Stir well and leave for 4 minutes. Pour through a fine sieve (strainer) into the ovenproof bowl.

3 Beat half the sugar with the egg yolks until light and fluffy. Sift the flour and ground ginger together and fold into the egg yolk mixture with the breadcrumbs and ground almonds.

4 Whisk the egg whites until stiff, then gradually whisk in the remaining caster sugar. Fold into the mixture, in two batches. Spoon into the ovenproof bowl and smooth the top.

5 Cover the bowl with a piece of pleated greased baking parchment and secure with string. Bake for 40 minutes, or until the sponge is firm to the touch. Turn out and serve immediately.

COOK'S TIP
This pudding can also be baked in a 900ml/1½ pint/3¾ cup loaf tin (pan) and served thickly sliced.

Energy 382Kcal/1617kJ; Protein 9.7g; Carbohydrate 70.6g, of which sugars 53.5g; Fat 8.9g, of which saturates 1.7g; Cholesterol 171mg; Calcium 93mg; Fibre 1g; Sodium 240mg.

STICKY TOFFEE PUDDING

FORGET THE MAIN COURSE BECAUSE THIS IS GOOEY AND GORGEOUS FOR A SWEET-COURSE-ONLY MEAL.

SERVES SIX

INGREDIENTS
    115g/4oz/1 cup toasted walnuts,
        chopped
    175g/6oz/¾ cup butter
    175g/6oz/scant 1 cup soft brown
        sugar
    60ml/4 tbsp double (heavy) cream
    30ml/2 tbsp lemon juice
    2 eggs, beaten
    115g/4oz/1 cup self-raising (self-
        rising) flour

1 Grease a 900ml/1½ pint/¾ cup
heatproof bowl and add half the nuts.

2 Heat 50g/2oz/4 tbsp of the butter
with 50g/2oz/4 tbsp of the sugar, the
cream and 15ml/1 tbsp lemon juice in a
small pan, stirring until smooth. Pour
half into the heatproof bowl, then swirl
to coat it a little way up the sides.

3 Beat the remaining butter and sugar
until fluffy, then beat in the eggs. Fold
in the flour, remaining nuts and lemon
juice and spoon into the basin.

4 Cover the bowl with baking
parchment with a pleat folded in the
centre, then tie securely with string.

5 Steam the pudding for about
1¼ hours, until set in the centre.

6 Just before serving, gently warm the
remaining sauce. Unmould the pudding
on to a warm plate and pour over the
warm sauce.

Energy 606Kcal/2523kJ; Protein 7.5g; Carbohydrate 46g, of which sugars 31.6g; Fat 44.9g, of which saturates 20.3g; Cholesterol 152mg; Calcium 122mg; Fibre 1.3g; Sodium 279mg.

CUSTARD

WHEN MAKING A CUSTARD, WHETHER YOU WANT A THIN POURING CUSTARD OR A THICK CUSTARD FOR A TRIFLE, ADDING A LITTLE CORNFLOUR WILL STABILIZE THE EGG AND HELP TO PREVENT CURDLING. THIS RECIPE USES A REASONABLE AMOUNT OF CORNFLOUR FOR SURE SUCCESS — SIMPLE TO MAKE AND SERIOUSLY COMFORTING TO EAT WITH ALL SORTS OF HEARTWARMING HOT PUDDINGS.

SERVES FOUR TO SIX

INGREDIENTS
   450ml/¾ pint/scant 2 cups milk
   few drops of vanilla extract
   2 eggs plus 1 egg yolk
   15ml/1 tbsp caster (superfine)
     sugar
   15ml/1 tbsp cornflour (cornstarch)
   30ml/2 tbsp water

1 In a pan heat the milk with the vanilla extract and remove from the heat just as the milk comes to the boil.

2 Whisk the eggs and yolk in a bowl with the caster sugar until well combined but not frothy. In a separate bowl, blend together the cornflour with the water and mix into the eggs. Whisk in a little of the hot milk, then mix in all the remaining milk.

COOK'S TIP
If you are not serving the custard immediately, cover the surface of the sauce with clear film (plastic wrap) to prevent a skin from forming and keep warm in a heatproof bowl over a pan of hot water.

3 Strain the egg and milk mixture back into the pan and heat gently, stirring frequently. Take care not to overheat the mixture or it will curdle.

4 Continue stirring until the custard thickens sufficiently to coat the back of a wooden spoon. Do not allow to boil or it will curdle. Serve immediately.

Energy 156Kcal/656kJ; Protein 8g; Carbohydrate 17.9g, of which sugars 11g; Fat 6.5g, of which saturates 2.4g; Cholesterol 170mg; Calcium 147mg; Fibre 0g; Sodium 92mg.

TRADITIONAL ENGLISH RICE PUDDING

MEMORIES OF SCHOOL-DAYS RICE PUDDING ARE EITHER THE BEST OR WORST AND THIS IS THE RECIPE FOR DESSERTS THAT FEATURE IN DAYDREAMS. A PROPER RICE PUDDING IS SMOOTH AND CREAMY WITH JUST A HINT OF FRAGRANT SPICES. SERVE IT WITH A SPOONFUL OF THICK CHERRY JAM, IF YOU LIKE.

SERVES FOUR

INGREDIENTS
    600ml/1 pint/2½ cups creamy milk
    1 vanilla pod (bean)
    50g/2oz/generous ¼ cup short grain
        pudding rice
    45ml/3 tbsp caster (superfine) sugar
    25g/1oz/2 tbsp butter
    freshly grated nutmeg

1 Pour the milk into a pan and add the vanilla pod. Bring to simmering point, then remove from the heat, cover and leave to infuse for 1 hour. Preheat the oven to 150°C/300°F/Gas 2.

2 Put the rice and sugar in an oven-proof dish. Strain the milk over the rice, discarding the vanilla pod. Stir to mix, then dot the surface with the butter.

3 Bake, uncovered, for 2 hours. After about 40 minutes, stir the surface skin into the pudding, and repeat this after a further 40 minutes. At this point, sprinkle the surface of the pudding with grated nutmeg. Allow the pudding to finish cooking without stirring.

COOK'S TIP
If possible, always use a non-stick pan when heating milk, otherwise it is likely to stick to the bottom of the pan and burn.

Energy 233Kcal/972kJ; Protein 5.9g; Carbohydrate 28.2g, of which sugars 18.6g; Fat 11.1g, of which saturates 7g; Cholesterol 34mg; Calcium 187mg; Fibre 0g; Sodium 103mg.

BAKED BANANAS <u>WITH</u> ICE CREAM

BAKED BANANAS MAKE THE PERFECT PARTNERS FOR DELICIOUS VANILLA ICE CREAM TOPPED WITH A TOASTED HAZELNUT SAUCE. THIS IS QUICK AND EASY FOR TIMES WHEN ONLY SWEET TREATS WILL DO.

SERVES FOUR

INGREDIENTS
    4 large bananas
    15ml/1 tbsp lemon juice
    4 large scoops vanilla ice cream
For the sauce
    25g/1oz/2 tbsp unsalted (sweet)
      butter
    50g/2oz/½ cup hazelnuts, toasted
      and roughly chopped
    45ml/3 tbsp golden (light corn) syrup
    30ml/2 tbsp lemon juice

1 Preheat the oven to 180°C/350°F/ Gas 4. Place the unpeeled bananas on a baking sheet and brush them with the lemon juice. Bake for about 20 minutes until the skins are turning black and the flesh gives a little when the bananas are gently squeezed.

2 Meanwhile, make the sauce. Melt the butter in a small pan. Add the hazelnuts and cook gently for 1 minute. Add the syrup and lemon juice and heat, stirring, for 1 minute more.

3 To serve, slit each banana open with a knife and open out the skins to reveal the tender flesh. Transfer to serving plates and serve with scoops of ice cream. Pour the sauce over.

Energy 382Kcal/1598kJ; Protein 5.4g; Carbohydrate 49.4g, of which sugars 45.7g; Fat 18.6g, of which saturates 7.6g; Cholesterol 28mg; Calcium 88mg; Fibre 2.1g; Sodium 106mg.

YORKSHIRE CURD TART

THE DISTINGUISHING FLAVOUR IN YORKSHIRE CURD TARTS IS ALLSPICE, OR "CLOVE PEPPER" AS IT WAS KNOWN LOCALLY. THIS TART IS SO GOOD THAT IT IS DIFFICULT TO RESIST SECOND HELPINGS.

2 Put the dough on a floured surface, knead lightly and briefly, then form into a ball. Roll out the pastry thinly and use to line a 20cm/8in fluted loose-based flan tin (tart pan). Cover with clear film (plastic wrap) and chill for about 15 minutes.

3 Preheat the oven to 190°C/375°F/ Gas 5. Mix the sugar with the ground allspice in a bowl, then stir in the eggs, lemon rind and juice, butter, curd cheese and raisins. Mix well.

4 Pour the filling into the pastry case, then bake for 40 minutes, or until the pastry is cooked and the filling is lightly set and golden brown. Cut the tart into wedges while it is still slightly warm, and serve with cream, if you like.

SERVES EIGHT

INGREDIENTS
   90g/3½oz/scant ½ cup soft light
      brown sugar
   large pinch of ground allspice
   3 eggs, beaten
   grated rind and juice of 1 lemon
   40g/1½oz/3 tbsp butter, melted
   450g/1lb/2 cups curd
      (farmer's) cheese
   75g/3oz/scant ½ cup raisins
For the pastry
   225g/8oz/2 cups plain
      (all-purpose) flour
   115g/4oz/½ cup butter, diced
   1 egg yolk
   15–30ml/1–2 tbsp chilled water

1 To make the pastry, place the flour in a large mixing bowl and rub or cut in the butter until the mixture resembles fine breadcrumbs. Stir the egg yolk into the flour and add just enough of the water to bind the mixture together to form a dough.

COOK'S TIP
Although it is not traditional, mixed spice (apple pie spice) would make a good substitute for the ground allspice.

Energy 406Kcal/1700kJ; Protein 14g; Carbohydrate 41.4g, of which sugars 20g; Fat 21.7g, of which saturates 12.4g; Cholesterol 159mg; Calcium 110mg; Fibre 1.1g; Sodium 371mg.

TREACLE TART

TRADITIONAL SHORTCRUST PASTRY IS PERFECT FOR THIS OLD-FASHIONED FAVOURITE, WITH ITS STICKY LEMON AND GOLDEN SYRUP FILLING AND TWISTED LATTICE TOPPING.

SERVES FOUR TO SIX

INGREDIENTS
  260g/9½oz/generous ¾ cup golden
    (light corn) syrup
  75g/3oz/1½ cups fresh
    white breadcrumbs
  grated rind of 1 lemon
  30ml/2 tbsp lemon juice
For the pastry
  150g/5oz/1¼ cups plain
    (all-purpose) flour
  2.5ml/½ tsp salt
  130g/4½oz/9 tbsp chilled
    butter, diced
  45–60/3–4 tbsp chilled water

1 To make the pastry, combine the flour and salt in a bowl. Rub or cut in the butter until the mixture resembles coarse breadcrumbs.

2 With a fork, stir in just enough water to bind the dough. Gather into a smooth ball, knead lightly for a few seconds until smooth then wrap in clear film (plastic wrap) and chill for at least 20 minutes.

3 On a lightly floured surface, roll out the pastry to a thickness of 3mm/⅛in. Transfer to a 20cm/8in fluted flan tin (tart pan) and trim off the overhang. Chill the pastry case for 20 minutes. Reserve the pastry trimmings.

4 Put a baking sheet in the oven and preheat to 200°C/400°F/Gas 6. To make the filling, warm the syrup in a pan until it melts.

5 Remove the syrup from the heat and stir in the breadcrumbs and lemon rind. Leave to stand for 10 minutes, then add more breadcrumbs if the mixture is too thin and moist. Stir in the lemon juice, then spread the mixture evenly in the pastry case.

6 Roll out the pastry trimmings and cut into 10–12 thin strips.

7 Twist the strips into spirals, then lay half of them on the filling. Arrange the remaining strips at right angles to form a lattice. Press the ends on to the rim.

8 Place the tart on the hot baking sheet and bake for 10 minutes. Lower the oven temperature to 190°C/375°F/ Gas 5. Bake for 15 minutes more, until golden. Serve warm with custard.

Energy 630Kcal/2646kJ; Protein 6.1g; Carbohydrate 95.2g, of which sugars 52.6g; Fat 27.6g, of which saturates 17g; Cholesterol 69mg; Calcium 93mg; Fibre 1.6g; Sodium 762mg.

BAKEWELL TART

This delicious, almond-rich tart is undoubtedly "baked well", but is actually named after the English village of Bakewell, where it originated.

SERVES FOUR

INGREDIENTS
    225g/8oz puff pastry
    30ml/2 tbsp raspberry or
      apricot jam
    2 eggs, plus 2 egg yolks
    115g/4oz/½ cup caster
      (superfine) sugar
    115g/4oz/½ cup butter, melted
    50g/2oz/⅔ cup ground almonds
    a few drops of almond extract
    icing (confectioners') sugar,
      for dusting

1 Preheat the oven to 200°C/400°F Gas 6. Roll out the pastry on a lightly floured surface and use to line an 18cm/7in pie plate. Trim the edge.

2 Re-roll the pastry trimmings and cut out wide strips of pastry. Use these to decorate the edge of the pastry case by gently twisting them around the rim, joining the strips together as necessary. Prick the pastry case all over, then spread the jam over the base.

3 Whisk the eggs, egg yolks and sugar together in a bowl until the mixture is thick and pale.

4 Gently stir the melted butter, ground almonds and almond extract into the whisked egg mixture.

5 Pour the mixture into the pastry case and bake for 30 minutes, or until the filling is just set and is lightly browned. Dust with icing sugar before serving hot, warm or cold.

COOK'S TIP
Since this pastry case is not baked blind before being filled, place a baking sheet in the oven while it preheats, then place the tart on the hot sheet. This will ensure that the base of the pastry case cooks right through.

Energy 417Kcal/1753kJ; Protein 8.6g; Carbohydrate 56.1g, of which sugars 36g; Fat 19.9g, of which saturates 1.7g; Cholesterol 215mg; Calcium 78mg; Fibre 0g; Sodium 226mg.

LEMON AND ALMOND TART

THIS REFRESHING, TANGY TART HAS A RICH, CREAMY LEMON FILLING SET OFF BY A CARAMELIZED SUGAR TOP. SERVE WARM OR COLD WITH A DOLLOP OF CRÈME FRAÎCHE OR NATURAL YOGURT.

SERVES EIGHT TO TEN

INGREDIENTS
  2 eggs
  50g/2oz/¼ cup golden caster
    (superfine) sugar
  finely grated rind and juice of
    4 unwaxed lemons
  2.5ml/½ tsp vanilla extract
  50g/2oz/½ cup ground almonds
  120ml/4fl oz/½ cup single (light)
    cream
  crème fraîche or natural (plain)
    yogurt, to serve
For the pastry
  225g/8oz/2 cups plain (all-purpose)
    flour
  75g/3oz/¾ cup icing (confectioners')
    sugar, plus extra for dusting
  130g/4½oz/9 tbsp butter
  1 egg, beaten
  a pinch of salt

1 Preheat the oven to 180°C/350°F/ Gas 4. To make the pastry, sift together the flour and sugar in a bowl. Rub in the butter with your fingers until the mixture resembles fine breadcrumbs. Add the egg and salt, then mix to a smooth dough.

2 Knead the dough lightly on a floured work surface and form into a smooth flat round. Wrap the dough in clear film (plastic wrap) and chill for 15 minutes.

3 Roll out the dough on a lightly floured work surface and use to line a 23cm/9in loose-bottomed flan tin (tart pan). Prick the pastry base and chill for a further 15 minutes.

4 Line the pastry case with baking parchment. Cover with baking beans and bake blind for 10 minutes. Remove the paper and beans and return the pastry case to the oven for a further 10 minutes or until it is light golden.

5 Meanwhile, make the filling. Beat the eggs with the sugar until the mixture leaves a thin ribbon trail. Gently stir in the lemon rind and juice, vanilla extract, almonds and cream.

6 Pour the filling into the pastry case and level the surface. Bake for about 25 minutes or until the filling is set.

7 Heat the grill (broiler) to high. Sift a thick layer of icing sugar over the tart and grill (broil) until it caramelizes.

8 Decorate the tart with a little extra sifted icing sugar before serving it warm or cold with generous dollops of crème fraîche or natural yogurt.

Energy 379Kcal/1583kJ; Protein 7.4g; Carbohydrate 39.1g, of which sugars 17.4g; Fat 22.6g, of which saturates 11.3g; Cholesterol 129mg; Calcium 87mg; Fibre 1.3g; Sodium 138mg.

MINCE PIES WITH ORANGE WHISKY BUTTER

MINCEMEAT GETS THE LUXURY TREATMENT WITH THE ADDITION OF GLACÉ CITRUS PEEL, CHERRIES AND WHISKY TO MAKE A MARVELLOUS FILLING FOR TRADITIONAL FESTIVE PIES. WHEN SEASONAL ACTIVITIES ARE ALL A BIT MUCH, TAKE TIME OUT TO RELAX OVER A COUPLE OF THESE SPIRIT-LIFTING PIES.

MAKES TWELVE TO FIFTEEN

INGREDIENTS
  225g/8oz/⅔ cup mincemeat
  50g/2oz/¼ cup glacé (candied) citrus
    peel, chopped
  50g/2oz/¼ cup glacé (candied)
    cherries, chopped
  30ml/2 tbsp whisky
  1 egg, beaten, or a little milk
  icing (confectioners') sugar,
    for dusting
For the pastry
  1 egg yolk
  5ml/1 tsp grated orange rind
  15ml/1 tbsp caster (superfine) sugar
  10ml/2 tsp chilled water
  225g/8oz/2 cups plain
    (all-purpose) flour
  150g/5oz/10 tbsp butter, diced
For the orange whisky butter
  75g/3oz/6 tbsp butter, softened
  175g/6oz/1½ cups icing
    (confectioners') sugar, sifted
  30ml/2 tbsp whisky
  5ml/1 tsp grated orange rind

1 To make the pastry, lightly beat the egg yolk in a bowl, then add the grated orange rind, caster sugar and water and mix together. Cover and set aside. Sift the flour into a separate mixing bowl.

VARIATIONS
• Use either puff or filo pastry instead of shortcrust for a change.
• Replace the whisky in both the filling and the flavoured butter with Cointreau or brandy, if you like.

2 Using your fingertips, rub the diced butter into the flour until the mixture resembles fine breadcrumbs. Stir in the egg mixture and mix to a dough. Wrap in clear film (plastic wrap) and chill for 30 minutes.

3 Mix together the mincemeat, glacé peel and cherries, then add the whisky.

4 Roll out three-quarters of the pastry. With a fluted pastry (cookie) cutter stamp out rounds and line 12–15 patty tins (muffin pans). Re-roll the trimmings thinly and stamp out star shapes.

5 Preheat the oven to 200°C/400°F/ Gas 6. Spoon a little filling into each pastry case (pie shell) and top with a star shape. Brush with a little beaten egg or milk and bake for 20–25 minutes, or until golden. Leave to cool.

6 Meanwhile, make the orange whisky butter. Place the softened butter, icing sugar, whisky and grated orange rind in a bowl and beat with a wooden spoon until light and fluffy.

7 To serve, lift off each pastry star, pipe a whirl of whisky butter on top of the filling, then replace the star. Lightly dust the mince pies with a little icing sugar.

COOK'S TIP
There is a wide range of small, shaped pastry cutters available from kitchenware stores and special seasonal packs with a festive theme also include stars and Christmas trees. While metal cutters are usually the wiser buy, as these will be used only annually, cheaper plastic cutters are fine.

Energy 356Kcal/1491kJ; Protein 2.9g; Carbohydrate 46.9g, of which sugars 32.4g; Fat 17.5g, of which saturates 10.1g; Cholesterol 77mg; Calcium 49mg; Fibre 1.1g; Sodium 140mg.

VANILLA CAFFÈ LATTE

THIS LUXURIOUS VANILLA AND CHOCOLATE VERSION OF THE CLASSIC COFFEE DRINK CAN BE SERVED AT ANY TIME OF THE DAY TOPPED WITH WHIPPED CREAM, WITH CINNAMON STICKS TO STIR AND FLAVOUR THE DRINK. CAFFÈ LATTE IS A POPULAR BREAKFAST DRINK IN ITALY AND FRANCE, AND IS NOW WIDELY AVAILABLE ELSEWHERE.

SERVES TWO

INGREDIENTS
　　700ml/1¼ pints/scant 3 cups milk
　　250ml/8fl oz/1 cup espresso or very
　　　strong coffee
　　45ml/3 tbsp vanilla sugar, plus extra
　　　to taste
　　115g/4oz dark (bittersweet)
　　　chocolate, grated

1 Pour the milk into a small pan and bring to the boil, then remove from the heat. Mix the espresso or very strong coffee with 500ml/16fl oz/2 cups of the boiled milk in a large heatproof jug (pitcher). Sweeten with vanilla sugar to taste.

2 Return the remaining boiled milk in the pan to the heat and add the 45ml/ 3 tbsp vanilla sugar. Stir constantly until dissolved. Bring to the boil, then reduce the heat. Add the dark chocolate and continue to heat, stirring constantly until all the chocolate has melted and the mixture is smooth and glossy.

3 Pour the chocolate milk into the jug of coffee and whisk thoroughly. Serve in tall mugs or glasses topped with whipped cream and with cinnamon sticks to stir.

Energy 543Kcal/2290kJ; Protein 14.9g; Carbohydrate 76.5g, of which sugars 76g; Fat 22.1g, of which saturates 13.4g; Cholesterol 24mg; Calcium 451mg; Fibre 1.5g; Sodium 156mg.

FROTHY HOT CHOCOLATE

REALLY GOOD HOT CHOCOLATE DOESN'T COME AS A POWDER IN A PACKET — IT IS MADE WITH THE BEST CHOCOLATE YOU CAN AFFORD, WHISKED IN HOT MILK UNTIL REALLY FROTHY. LARGE MUGS ARE ESSENTIAL FOR PLENTY OF ROOM TO ACCOMMODATE THE LIP-SMACKINGLY GOOD FROTH AS WELL AS THE DARK, RICH CHOCOLATE UNDERNEATH. THIS IS TRUE COMFORT IN A MUG.

SERVES FOUR

INGREDIENTS

   1 litre/1¾ pints/4 cups milk
   1 vanilla pod (bean)
   50–115g/2–4oz dark (bittersweet)
     chocolate, grated

1 Pour the milk into a pan. Split the vanilla pod lengthways using a sharp knife to reveal the seeds, and add it to the milk; the vanilla seeds and the pod will flavour the milk.

2 Add the chocolate. The amount to use depends on personal taste — start with a smaller amount if you are unsure of the flavour and taste at the beginning of step 3, adding more if necessary.

3 Heat the chocolate milk gently, stirring until all the chocolate has melted and the mixture is smooth, then whisk with a wire whisk until the mixture boils. Remove the vanilla pod from the pan and divide the drink among four mugs or heatproof glasses. Serve the hot chocolate immediately.

Energy 179Kcal/755kJ; Protein 9.1g; Carbohydrate 19.7g, of which sugars 19.6g; Fat 7.8g, of which saturates 4.8g; Cholesterol 16mg; Calcium 304mg; Fibre 0.3g; Sodium 108mg.

HOT TODDY

HOT TODDIES ARE NORMALLY MADE WITH WHISKY BUT RUM WORKS REALLY WELL TOO AND PRODUCES A DELICIOUSLY WARMING DRINK THAT'S PERFECT FOR A COLD WINTER EVENING – OR EVEN A WINTER AFTERNOON AFTER A HEARTY WALK OUT IN THE FREEZING COLD COUNTRYSIDE. YOU CAN ALSO FLAVOUR THIS TODDY WITH DIFFERENT SPICES SUCH AS A VANILLA POD (BEAN) OR CINNAMON STICK.

SERVES FOUR

INGREDIENTS
    300ml/½ pint/1¼ cups
      dark rum
    45ml/3 tbsp caster (superfine)
      sugar
    1 star anise

1 Pour the rum into a heatproof jug (pitcher) and add the sugar and star anise. Pour in 450ml/¾ pint/scant 2 cups boiling water and stir thoroughly until the sugar has dissolved.

2 Carefully pour the hot toddy into heatproof glasses or mugs and serve immediately.

Energy 211Kcal/878kJ; Protein 0.1g; Carbohydrate 11.8g, of which sugars 11.8g; Fat 0g, of which saturates 0g; Cholesterol 0mg; Calcium 6mg; Fibre 0g; Sodium 1mg.

COFFEE EGG-NOG

CHILL OUT WHEN THE AFTERNOON HEAT TURNS TO STRESS AND SIP THIS RATHER SPECIAL GROWN-UP COFFEE DRINK, WHICH IS PARTICULARLY SUITABLE FOR DAYTIME SUMMER-HOLIDAY FESTIVITIES.

SERVES SIX TO EIGHT

INGREDIENTS
   8 eggs, separated
   225g/8oz sugar
   250ml/8fl oz cold strong coffee
      (espresso strength or filter/cafetière
      (press pot) brewed at 75g/3oz
      coffee per 1 litre/1¾ pints/4 cups
      water)
   220ml/7½fl oz Scotch or bourbon
   220ml/7½fl oz double (heavy) cream
   120ml/4fl oz whipped cream
   ground nutmeg, to decorate

1 Thoroughly beat the egg yolks, then add the sugar mixing well.

2 Heat the egg mixture gently in a pan over a low heat, stirring with a wooden spoon. Allow to cool a few minutes, stir in the coffee and whisky, and then slowly add the cream, stirring well.

3 Beat the egg whites until stiff and stir into the egg-nog, mixing well. Pour into small round cups, top each with a small dollop of whipped cream and sprinkle nutmeg on top.

Energy 605Kcal/2519kJ; Protein 11.2g; Carbohydrate 40.4g, of which sugars 40.4g; Fat 36.6g, of which saturates 19.8g; Cholesterol 376mg; Calcium 95mg; Fibre 0g; Sodium 127mg.

IRISH CHOCOLATE VELVET

THIS IS A LUXURIOUS CREAMY HOT CHOCOLATE DRINK, WITH JUST A TOUCH OF ALCOHOL TO FORTIFY IT. IT WOULD BE THE PERFECT ANTIDOTE TO A BOUT OF FLAGGING WINTER SPIRITS.

SERVES FOUR

INGREDIENTS
   250ml/8fl oz/1 cup double (heavy)
      cream
   400ml/14fl oz milk
   115g/4oz milk chocolate,
      chopped into small pieces
   30ml/2 tbsp unsweetened
      cocoa powder
   60ml/4 tbsp Irish whiskey
   whipped cream, for topping
   chocolate curls, to decorate

1 Whip half the cream in a bowl until it is thick enough to hold its shape.

2 Place the milk and chocolate in a heavy based pan and heat gently, stirring all the time, until the chocolate has melted. Whisk in the cocoa, then bring to the boil.

3 Remove from the heat and stir in the remaining cream and the Irish whiskey. Pour into four warmed heatproof mugs or glasses and top each serving with a generous spoonful of the whipped cream, finishing with a garnish of milk chocolate curls.

Energy 559Kcal/2321kJ; Protein 7.2g; Carbohydrate 24.9g, of which sugars 23.8g; Fat 45g, of which saturates 27.7g; Cholesterol 93mg; Calcium 170mg; Fibre 1.6g; Sodium 130mg.

Teatime Treats, Cakes and Breads

Baking is wholesome and satisfying. Wafts of sweet baking aromas are uplifting and tease the senses. From the mixing, beating or kneading through to enjoying the results, baking is wonderfully therapeutic in the process as well as in the result.

DANISH PASTRIES

EVEN THOUGH THESE WORLD-FAMOUS PASTRIES ARE TIME-CONSUMING TO MAKE, THE PROCESS IS ENJOYABLE AND THE RESULTS ARE INCOMPARABLY WONDERFUL, ESPECIALLY WITH THE COFFEE FILLING.

MAKES SIXTEEN

INGREDIENTS
45ml/3 tbsp near-boiling water
30ml/2 tbsp ground coffee
40g/1½oz/3 tbsp butter
115g/4oz/½ cup caster
  (superfine) sugar
1 egg yolk
115g/4oz/1 cup ground almonds
1 egg, beaten
275g/10oz/1 cup apricot jam (jelly)
30ml/2 tbsp water
175g/6oz/1½ cups icing
  (confectioners') sugar
50g/2oz/½ cup flaked (sliced)
  almonds, toasted
50g/2oz/¼ cup glacé
  (candied) cherries
For the pastry
275g/10oz/2½ cups plain
  (all-purpose) flour
1.5ml/¼ tsp salt
15g/½oz/1 tbsp caster
  (superfine) sugar
225g/8oz/1 cup butter, softened
10ml/2 tsp easy-blend (rapid-rise)
  dried yeast
1 egg, beaten
100ml/3½fl oz/scant ½ cup chilled
  water

1 To make the pastry, sift the flour, salt and sugar into a bowl. Rub in 25g/1oz/2 tbsp butter. Stir in the yeast. In a separate bowl, mix the egg and water together, add to the flour mixture and mix to a soft dough. Lightly knead for 4–5 minutes. Place in a plastic bag, seal and chill for 15 minutes.

2 Put the remaining butter for the pastry between two sheets of baking parchment and beat with a rolling pin to make an 18cm/7in square. Chill.

3 Roll out the dough on a floured surface to a 25cm/10in square. Put the butter in the middle of the dough square, angled like a diamond, then bring up each corner of the dough to enclose it fully.

4 Roll out the pastry thinly to measure about 35cm/14in in length. Turn up the bottom third of the pastry, then gently fold down the top third. Seal the edges together with a rolling pin. Wrap the pastry in clear film (plastic wrap) and chill for 15 minutes.

5 Repeat the rolling and folding three more times, turning the pastry after folding over so that the short ends are at the top and bottom. Allow the pastry a 15-minute rest between each turn.

6 To make the filling, pour the hot water over the coffee and infuse for 4 minutes. Strain through a fine sieve. Cream the butter and sugar together. Beat in the egg yolk, ground almonds and 15ml/1 tbsp of the coffee.

7 Divide the dough and filling equally into three. Roll one dough portion to an 18 × 35cm/7 × 14in rectangle. Spread with filling and roll up from a short end. Cut into six equal slices. Roll another portion into a 25cm/10in round, and cut into six equal segments.

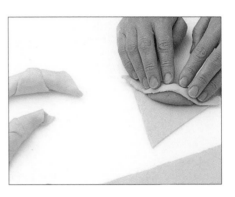

8 Put a spoonful of filling at the widest end of each segment. Roll the pastry towards its point to form a crescent.

9 Roll out the remaining dough into a 20cm/8in square; cut into four. Place some filling in the centre of each piece, and shape by making cuts from each corner almost to the centre, then fold four alternate points to the centre.

10 Preheat the oven to 220°C/425°F/Gas 7. Space the pastries well apart on greased baking sheets. Cover loosely with oiled clear film and leave to rise for about 20 minutes, until almost doubled in size. Brush with the egg and bake for 15–20 minutes until lightly browned and crisp. Cool on wire racks.

11 Put the jam in a pan with the water; bring to the boil, then sieve. Brush the jam over the warm pastries. Mix the icing sugar with the remaining coffee to make a thick icing. Drizzle the icing over some of the pastries and decorate some with almonds or chopped glacé cherries. Leave to set before serving.

Energy 387Kcal/1623kJ; Protein 5.1g; Carbohydrate 48.1g, of which sugars 34.6g; Fat 20.8g, of which saturates 9.4g; Cholesterol 76mg; Calcium 65mg; Fibre 1.3g; Sodium 161mg.

CROISSANTS

PERFECT CROISSANTS CONSIST OF PUFFED AND FLAKY LAYERS OF YEAST DOUGH. THEIR PREPARATION, WHICH IS A SOOTHING, CREATIVE PROCESS, IS NOT TO BE RUSHED; EATING THEM IS BREAKFAST BLISS.

MAKES FOURTEEN

INGREDIENTS
  350g/12oz/3 cups unbleached strong white bread flour
  115g/4oz/1 cup fine plain (all-purpose) flour, preferably French
  5ml/1 tsp salt
  25g/1oz/2 tbsp caster (superfine) sugar
  15g/½ oz fresh yeast
  225ml/scant 8fl oz/scant 1 cup lukewarm milk
  1 egg, lightly beaten
  225g/8oz/1 cup butter
For the glaze
  1 egg yolk
  15ml/1 tbsp milk

COOK'S TIP
Make sure that the block of butter and the dough are about the same temperature when combining, to ensure the best results.

VARIATION
To make chocolate-filled croissants, place a small square of milk or plain (semisweet) chocolate or 15ml/1 tbsp coarsely chopped chocolate at the wide end of each triangle before rolling up as in step 8.

1 Sift the flours and salt together into a large bowl. Stir in the sugar. Make a well in the centre. Cream the yeast with 45ml/3 tbsp of the milk, then stir in the remainder. Add the yeast mixture to the centre of the flour, then add the egg and gradually beat in the flour until it forms a dough.

2 Turn out on to a lightly floured surface and knead for 3–4 minutes. Place in a large lightly oiled bowl, cover with lightly oiled clear film (plastic wrap) and leave in a warm place, for about 45–60 minutes, or until doubled in bulk.

3 Knock back (punch down), re-cover and chill for 1 hour. Meanwhile, flatten the butter into a block about 2cm/¾in thick. Knock back the dough and turn out on to a lightly floured surface. Roll out into a rough 25cm/10in square, rolling the edges thinner than the centre.

4 Place the block of butter diagonally in the centre and fold the corners of the dough over the butter like an envelope, tucking in the edges to completely enclose the butter.

5 Roll the dough into a rectangle about 2cm/¾in thick and approximately twice as long as it is wide. Fold the bottom third up and the top third down and seal the edges with a rolling pin. Wrap the dough in clear film and chill for about 20 minutes.

6 Repeat the rolling, folding and chilling twice more, turning the dough by 90 degrees each time. Roll out on a floured surface into a 63 x 33cm/25 x 13in rectangle; trim the edges to leave a 60 x 30cm/24 x 12in rectangle. Cut in half lengthways. Cut crossways into 14 equal triangles with 15cm/6in bases.

7 Place the dough triangles on two baking sheets, cover with clear film and chill for 10 minutes.

8 To shape the croissants, place each one with the wide end at the top, hold each side and pull gently to stretch the top of the triangle a little, then roll towards the point, finishing with the pointed end tucked underneath. Curve the ends towards the pointed end to make a crescent. Place on two baking sheets, spaced well apart.

9 Mix together the egg yolk and milk for the glaze. Lightly brush a little glaze over the croissants, avoiding the cut edges of the dough. Cover the croissants loosely with lightly oiled clear film and leave to rise, in a warm place, for about 30 minutes, or until they are nearly doubled in size.

10 Meanwhile, preheat the oven to 220°C/425°F/Gas 7. Brush the croissants with the remaining glaze and bake for 15–20 minutes, or until crisp and golden. Transfer to a wire rack and leave to cool. The croissants are best served warm, with butter, if liked, and good quality fruit conserve.

Energy 253Kcal/1059kJ; Protein 4.3g; Carbohydrate 28.5g, of which sugars 3.2g; Fat 14.4g, of which saturates 8.7g; Cholesterol 50mg; Calcium 72mg; Fibre 1g; Sodium 251mg.

CINNAMON RINGS

THESE SPICY LITTLE MEXICAN PUFFS ARE AUTHENTICALLY CALLED BUÑUELOS. *THEY RESEMBLE MINIATURE DOUGHNUTS AND TASTE SO GOOD IT IS HARD NOT TO OVER-INDULGE. MAKE THEM FOR A SNACK OR AS A PICK-ME-UP TO SERVE WITH COFFEE OR TEA.*

MAKES TWELVE

INGREDIENTS
  225g/8oz/2 cups plain (all-purpose)
    flour
  pinch of salt
  5ml/1 tsp baking powder
  2.5ml/½ tsp ground anise
  115g/4oz/½ cup caster (superfine)
    sugar
  1 large (US extra large) egg
  120ml/4fl oz/½ cup milk
  50g/2oz/¼ cup butter
  oil, for deep-frying
  10ml/2 tsp ground cinnamon
  cinnamon sticks, to decorate

1 Sift the flour, salt, baking powder and ground anise into a mixing bowl. Add 30ml/2 tbsp of the caster sugar.

2 Place the egg and milk in a small jug (pitcher) and whisk well with a fork. Melt the butter in a small pan.

COOK'S TIP
Buñuelos are sometimes served with syrup for dunking, which is just right when you need cheering up. For a syrup heat 175g/6oz/¾ cup soft dark brown sugar and 450ml/¾ pint/scant 2 cups water. Add a cinnamon stick and stir until the sugar dissolves, then boil and simmer for 15 minutes without stirring. Cool slightly before serving.

3 Pour the egg mixture and milk gradually into the flour, stirring all the time, until well blended, then add the melted butter. Mix first with a wooden spoon and then with your hands to make a soft dough.

4 Lightly flour a work surface, tip the dough out on to it and knead for about 10 minutes, until smooth.

5 Divide the dough into 12 pieces and roll into balls. Slightly flatten each ball with your hand and then make a hole in the centre with the floured handle of a wooden spoon.

6 Heat the oil for deep frying to a temperature of 190°C/375°F, or until a cube of dried bread, added to the oil, floats and then turns a golden colour in 30–60 seconds. Fry the *buñuelos* in small batches until they are puffy and golden brown, turning them once or twice during cooking. As soon as they are golden, lift them out of the oil using a slotted spoon and lie them on a double layer of kitchen paper to drain.

7 Mix the remaining caster sugar with the ground cinnamon in a small bowl. Add the *buñuelos*, one at a time, while they are still warm, toss them in the mixture until they are lightly coated and either serve at once or leave to cool. Decorate with cinnamon sticks.

Energy 195Kcal/818kJ; Protein 2.6g; Carbohydrate 23.5g, of which sugars 10.8g; Fat 10.8g, of which saturates 3.2g; Cholesterol 29mg; Calcium 44mg; Fibre 0.5g; Sodium 38mg.

CHEWY FLAPJACK BARS

INSTEAD OF BUYING CEREAL BARS, THESE ARE EASY, FAR MORE TASTY AND MORE NUTRITIOUS THAN BOUGHT TYPES. GOOD FOR YOUR BODY AS WELL AS YOUR SPIRITS, THEY WILL KEEP IN AN AIRTIGHT CONTAINER FOR UP TO FOUR DAYS BUT ARE USUALLY EATEN FAR QUICKER THAN THAT.

MAKES TWELVE

INGREDIENTS
270g/10oz jar apple sauce
115g/4oz/½ cup ready-to-eat dried apricots, chopped
115g/4oz/¾ cup raisins
50g/2oz/¼ cup demerara (raw) sugar
50g/2oz/⅓ cup sunflower seeds
25g/1oz/2 tbsp sesame seeds
25g/1oz/¼ cup pumpkin seeds
75g/3oz/scant 1 cup rolled oats
75g/3oz/⅔ cup self-raising (self-rising) wholemeal (whole-wheat) flour
50g/2oz/⅔ cup desiccated (dry unsweetened shredded) coconut
2 eggs

1 Preheat the oven to 200°C/400°F/Gas 6. Grease a 20cm/8in square shallow baking tin (pan) and line with baking parchment.

2 Put the apple sauce in a large bowl with the apricots, raisins, sugar and the sunflower, sesame and pumpkin seeds and stir together with a wooden spoon until thoroughly mixed.

3 Add the oats, flour, coconut and eggs to the fruit mixture and gently stir together until evenly combined.

4 Turn the mixture into the tin and spread to the edges in an even layer. Bake for about 25 minutes or until golden and just firm to the touch.

5 Leave to cool in the tin, then lift out on to a board and cut into bars.

COOK'S TIP
Allow the baking parchment to hang over the edges of the tin; this makes baked bars easier to remove.

Energy 194Kcal/816kJ; Protein 4.8g; Carbohydrate 28.9g, of which sugars 18.7g; Fat 7.4g, of which saturates 2.9g; Cholesterol 31mg; Calcium 52mg; Fibre 2.6g; Sodium 48mg.

PECAN TOFFEE SHORTBREAD

COFFEE SHORTBREAD TOPPED WITH PECAN-STUDDED TOFFEE IS JUST DIVINE ... AND NUTS ARE VERY GOOD FOR YOU. CORNFLOUR GIVES A LIGHT TEXTURE, BUT ALL PLAIN FLOUR CAN BE USED INSTEAD.

MAKES TWENTY

INGREDIENTS
    15ml/1 tbsp ground coffee
    15ml/1 tbsp nearly boiling water
    115g/4oz/8 tbsp butter, softened
    30ml/2 tbsp smooth peanut butter
    75g/3oz/scant ½ cup caster
        (superfine) sugar
    75g/3oz/⅔ cup cornflour (cornstarch)
    185g/6½oz/1⅔ cups plain (all-
        purpose) flour
For the topping
    175g/6oz/12 tbsp butter
    175g/6oz/¾ cup soft light
        brown sugar
    30ml/2 tbsp golden (light corn) syrup
    175g/6oz/1 cup shelled pecan nuts,
        roughly chopped

1 Preheat the oven to 180°C/350°F/ Gas 4. Lightly grease and line the base of a 18 x 28cm/7 x 11in tin (pan) with baking parchment.

2 Put the coffee in a bowl and pour the hot water over. Leave to infuse for 4 minutes, then strain through a fine sieve (strainer).

3 Cream the butter, peanut butter, sugar and coffee together until light. Sift the cornflour and flour together and mix in to make a smooth dough.

4 Press into the base of the tin and prick all over with a fork. Bake for 20 minutes. To make the topping, put the butter, sugar and syrup in a pan and heat until melted. Bring to the boil.

5 Allow to simmer for 5 minutes, then stir in the chopped nuts. Spread the topping over the base. Leave in the tin until cold, then cut into fingers. Remove from the tin and serve.

Energy 278Kcal/1160kJ; Protein 2.3g; Carbohydrate 25.7g, of which sugars 15g; Fat 19.2g, of which saturates 8.3g; Cholesterol 31mg; Calcium 29mg; Fibre 0.8g; Sodium 102mg.

OATY CHOCOLATE-CHIP COOKIES

THESE CRUNCHY COOKIES ARE EASY ENOUGH FOR CHILDREN TO MAKE AND ARE SURE TO DISAPPEAR AS SOON AS THEY ARE BAKED. COOK WITH THE CHILDREN TO CREATE THEIR FUTURE COMFORT FOOD.

MAKES ABOUT TWENTY

INGREDIENTS
   115g/4oz/½ cup butter, plus extra
      for greasing
   115g/4oz/½ cup soft dark brown
      sugar
   2 eggs, lightly beaten
   45ml/3 tbsp milk
   5ml/1 tsp vanilla extract
   150g/5oz/1¼ cups plain (all-
      purpose) flour
   5ml/1 tsp baking powder
pinch of salt
   115g/4oz/generous 1 cup
      rolled oats
   175g/6oz plain (semisweet) chocolate
      chips
   115g/4oz/1 cup pecan nuts, chopped

1 Cream the butter and sugar in a large bowl until pale and fluffy. Add the beaten eggs, milk and vanilla extract, and beat thoroughly.

2 Sift in the flour, baking powder and salt, and stir in until well mixed. Fold in the rolled oats, chocolate chips and chopped pecan nuts.

3 Chill the mixture for at least 1 hour. Preheat the oven to 180°C/350°F/Gas 4. Grease two large baking trays.

4 Using two teaspoons, place mounds well apart on the trays and flatten with a spoon or fork. Bake for 10–12 minutes until the edges are just colouring, then cool on wire racks.

Energy 208Kcal/871kJ; Protein 3.3g; Carbohydrate 22.1g, of which sugars 12g; Fat 12.5g, of which saturates 5g; Cholesterol 36mg; Calcium 30mg; Fibre 1.1g; Sodium 47mg.

GIANT TRIPLE CHOCOLATE COOKIES

HERE IS THE ULTIMATE COOKIE. PACKED WITH CHOCOLATE AND MACADAMIA NUTS, EACH COOKIE IS A SUPER-STRESS BUSTER. YOU WILL HAVE TO BE PATIENT WHEN THEY COME OUT OF THE OVEN, AS THEY ARE TOO SOFT TO MOVE UNTIL COMPLETELY COLD: THAT'S STRESS ENOUGH TO DESERVE AT LEAST TWO!

MAKES TWELVE LARGE COOKIES

INGREDIENTS

90g/3½oz milk chocolate
90g/3½oz white chocolate
300g/11oz dark (bittersweet) chocolate (minimum 70 per cent cocoa solids)
90g/3½oz/7 tbsp unsalted (sweet) butter, at room temperature, diced
5ml/1 tsp vanilla extract
150g/5oz/¾ cup light muscovado (brown) sugar
150g/5oz/1¼ cups self-raising (self-rising) flour
100g/3½oz/scant 1 cup macadamia nut halves

1 Preheat the oven to 180°C/350°F/Gas 4. Line two baking sheets with baking parchment. Coarsely chop the milk and white chocolate and put them in a bowl.

2 Chop 200g/7oz of the dark chocolate into very large chunks, at least 2cm/¾in in size. Set aside.

3 Break up the remaining dark chocolate and place in a heatproof bowl set over a pan of barely simmering water. Stir until melted and smooth. Remove from the heat and stir in the butter, then the vanilla extract and muscovado sugar.

4 Add the flour and mix gently. Add half the dark chocolate chunks, all the milk and white chocolate and the nuts and fold together.

5 Spoon 12 mounds on to the baking sheets. Press the remaining dark chocolate chunks into the top of each cookie. Bake for about 12 minutes until just beginning to colour. Cool on the baking sheets.

Energy 413Kcal/1727kJ; Protein 3.9g; Carbohydrate 48.4g, of which sugars 38.6g; Fat 24g, of which saturates 11.6g; Cholesterol 18mg; Calcium 69mg; Fibre 1.8g; Sodium 117mg.

CHOCOLATE POTATO CAKE

ANONYMOUS MASHED POTATO MAKES THIS RICH CAKE ESPECIALLY MOIST AND DELICIOUS. USE A GOOD-QUALITY DARK CHOCOLATE FOR BEST RESULTS AND SERVE WITH WHIPPED CREAM.

MAKES ONE 23CM/9IN CAKE

INGREDIENTS
 oil, for greasing
 200g/7oz/1 cup sugar
 250g/9oz/1 cup and 2 tbsp butter
 4 eggs, separated
 275g/10oz dark (bittersweet)
   chocolate
 75g/3oz/¾ cup ground almonds
 165g/5½oz mashed potato
 225g/8oz/2 cups self-raising (self-
   rising) flour
 5ml/1 tsp cinnamon
 45ml/3 tbsp milk
 white and dark (bittersweet)
   chocolate shavings, to decorate
 whipped cream, to serve

1 Preheat the oven to 180°C/350°F/ Gas 4. Grease and line a 23cm/9in round cake tin (pan) with baking parchment.

2 In a bowl, cream together the sugar and 225g/8oz/1 cup of the butter until light and fluffy. Then beat the egg yolks into the creamed mixture one at a time, until it is smooth and creamy.

3 Finely chop or grate 175g/6oz of the chocolate and stir it into the creamed mixture with the ground almonds. Pass the mashed potato through a sieve or ricer and stir it into the creamed chocolate mixture.

4 Sift together the flour and cinnamon and fold into the mixture with the milk.

COOK'S TIP
Chocolate can be melted very successfully in the microwave. Place the pieces of chocolate in a plastic bowl. The chocolate may scorch if placed in a glass bowl. Microwave on high for 1 minute, stir, and then heat again for up to 1 minute, checking halfway through to see if it is done.

5 Whisk the egg whites until they hold stiff but not dry peaks, and fold into the cake mixture.

6 Spoon into the prepared tin and smooth over the top, but make a slight hollow in the middle to help keep the surface of the cake level during cooking. Bake in the oven for 1¼ hours until a wooden toothpick inserted in the centre comes out clean. Allow the cake to cool slightly in the tin, then turn out and cool on a wire rack.

7 Meanwhile break up the remaining chocolate into a heatproof bowl and stand it over a pan of hot water. Add the remaining butter in small pieces and stir well until the chocolate has melted and the mixture is smooth and glossy.

8 Peel off the lining paper and trim the top of the cake so that it is level. Smooth over the chocolate icing and allow to set. Decorate with white and dark chocolate shavings and serve with lashings of whipped cream.

Energy 5749Kcal/24034kJ; Protein 87.1g; Carbohydrate 590.9g, of which sugars 391.8g; Fat 354.8g, of which saturates 188.1g; Cholesterol 1465mg; Calcium 1408mg; Fibre 21.5g; Sodium 2731mg.

CHOCOLATE CHEESECAKE BROWNIES

A VERY DENSE CHOCOLATE BROWNIE MIXTURE IS SWIRLED WITH CREAMY CHEESECAKE MIXTURE TO GIVE A MARBLED EFFECT. CUT INTO TINY SQUARES FOR LITTLE MOUTHFULS OF ABSOLUTE HEAVEN.

MAKES SIXTEEN

INGREDIENTS
For the cheesecake mixture
   1 egg
   225g/8oz/1 cup full-fat
     cream cheese
   50g/2oz/¼ cup caster
     (superfine) sugar
   5ml/1 tsp vanilla essence (extract)
For the brownie mixture
   115g/4oz dark (bittersweet)
     chocolate (minimum 70 per cent
     cocoa solids)
   115g/4oz/½ cup unsalted
     (sweet) butter
   150g/5oz/¾ cup light muscovado
     (brown) sugar
   2 eggs, beaten
   50g/2oz/½ cup plain (all-purpose)
     flour

1 Preheat the oven to 160°C/325°F/ Gas 3. Line the base and sides of a 20cm/8in round cake tin (pan) with baking parchment.

2 To make the cheesecake mixture, beat the egg in a mixing bowl, then add the cream cheese, caster sugar and vanilla essence. Beat together until smooth and creamy.

3 To make the brownie mixture, melt the chocolate and butter together in the microwave or in a heatproof bowl set over a pan of gently simmering water. When the mixture is melted, remove from the heat, stir well, then add the sugar. Gradually pour in the beaten eggs, a little at a time, and beat well until thoroughly combined. Gently stir in the flour.

4 Spread two-thirds of the brownie mixture over the base of the tin. Spread the cheesecake mixture on top, then spoon on the remaining brownie mixture in heaps. Using a skewer, swirl the mixtures together.

5 Bake for 30–35 minutes, or until just set in the centre. Leave to cool in the tin, then cut into squares.

Energy 228Kcal/952kJ; Protein 2.6g; Carbohydrate 20.1g, of which sugars 17.7g; Fat 15.9g, of which saturates 9.5g; Cholesterol 72mg; Calcium 35mg; Fibre 0.3g; Sodium 103mg.

WHITE CHOCOLATE BROWNIES

THESE IRRESISTIBLE BROWNIES ARE PACKED FULL OF CREAMY WHITE CHOCOLATE AND JUICY DRIED FRUIT. THEY ARE BEST SERVED CUT INTO VERY SMALL PORTIONS AS THEY ARE INCREDIBLY RICH.

MAKES EIGHTEEN

INGREDIENTS

75g/3oz/6 tbsp unsalted (sweet)
  butter, diced
400g/14oz white chocolate, chopped
3 eggs
90g/3½oz/½ cup golden caster
  (superfine) sugar
10ml/2 tsp vanilla essence (extract)
90g/3½oz/¾ cup sultanas
  (golden raisins)
coarsely grated rind of 1 lemon, plus
  15ml/1 tbsp juice
200g/7oz/1¾ cups plain
  (all-purpose) flour

1 Preheat the oven to 190°C/375°F/ Gas 5. Grease and line a 28 x 20cm/ 11 x 8in shallow baking tin (pan) with baking parchment.

2 Put the butter and 300g/11oz of the chocolate in a bowl and melt over a pan of gently simmering water, stirring frequently.

3 Remove from the heat and beat in the eggs and sugar, then add the vanilla essence, sultanas, lemon rind and juice, flour and the remaining chocolate.

4 Turn the mixture into the tin and spread into the corners. Bake for about 20 minutes until slightly risen and the surface is only just turning golden. The centre should still be slightly soft. Leave to cool in the tin.

5 Cut the brownies into small squares and remove from the tin.

Energy 235Kcal/984kJ; Protein 4.3g; Carbohydrate 30.3g, of which sugars 21.8g; Fat 11.6g, of which saturates 6.6g; Cholesterol 47mg; Calcium 88mg; Fibre 0.4g; Sodium 65mg.

CHOCOLATE ECLAIRS

MANY OF THE ÉCLAIRS SOLD IN FRENCH CAKE SHOPS ARE FILLED WITH CRÈME PÂTISSIÈRE. HERE, THE CRISP CHOUX PASTRY FINGERS ARE FILLED WITH FRESH CREAM, SLIGHTLY SWEETENED AND FLAVOURED WITH VANILLA, AND THE ÉCLAIRS ARE THICKLY COATED IN DARK CHOCOLATE.

MAKES TWELVE

INGREDIENTS
   300ml/½ pint/1¼ cups double
     (heavy) cream
   10ml/2 tsp icing (confectioners')
     sugar, sifted
   1.5ml/¼ tsp vanilla extract
   115g/4oz plain (semisweet)
     chocolate
   30ml/2 tbsp water
   25g/1oz/2 tbsp butter
For the pastry
   65g/2½oz/9 tbsp plain
     (all-purpose) flour
   pinch of salt
   50g/2oz/¼ cup butter, diced
   150ml/¼ pint/⅔ cup water
   2 eggs, lightly beaten

1 Preheat the oven to 200°C/400°F/ Gas 6. Grease a large baking sheet and line with baking parchment. To make the pastry, sift the flour and salt on to a small sheet of baking parchment. Heat the butter and water in a pan very gently until the butter melts.

2 Increase the heat and bring to a rolling boil. Remove the pan from the heat and immediately tip in all the flour. Beat vigorously with a wooden spoon until the flour is mixed into the liquid.

COOK'S TIP
When melting the chocolate, ensure that the bowl does not touch the hot water and keep the heat low. If the chocolate gets too hot, it will become unworkable.

3 Return the pan to a low heat, then beat the mixture until it leaves the sides of the pan and forms a ball. Set the pan aside and allow to cool for 2–3 minutes.

4 Add the beaten eggs, a little at a time, beating well after each addition, until you have a smooth, shiny paste, which is thick enough to hold its shape.

5 Spoon the choux pastry into a piping (pastry) bag fitted with a 2.5cm/1in plain nozzle. Pipe 10cm/4in lengths on to the prepared baking sheet. Use a wet knife to cut off the pastry at the nozzle.

6 Bake for 25–30 minutes, or until the pastries are well risen and golden brown. Remove from the oven and make a neat slit along the side of each to release the steam. Lower the oven temperature to 180°C/350°F/Gas 4 and bake for a further 5 minutes. Cool on a wire rack.

7 To make the filling, whip the cream with the icing sugar and vanilla extract until it just holds its shape. Spoon into a piping bag fitted with a 1cm/½in plain nozzle and use to fill the éclairs.

8 Place the chocolate and water in a small bowl set over a pan of hot water. Melt, stirring until smooth. Remove from the heat and gradually stir in the butter.

9 Carefully dip the top of each éclair in the melted chocolate, then place on a wire rack. Leave in a cool place until the chocolate is set. The éclairs are best served within 2 hours of being made, but they can be stored in the refrigerator for up to 24 hours.

Energy 253Kcal/1046kJ; Protein 2.7g; Carbohydrate 10.8g, of which sugars 6.5g; Fat 22.4g, of which saturates 13.5g; Cholesterol 86mg; Calcium 30mg; Fibre 0.4g; Sodium 58mg.

GREEK HONEY CRUNCH CREAMS

WITH ITS SCENT OF LIQUORICE AND ANISEED, GREEK HONEY LENDS A WONDERFUL FLAVOUR TO THESE COOKIES. IF YOU LIKE YOUR HONEY LESS STRONG, TRY USING ORANGE BLOSSOM OR LAVENDER INSTEAD.

MAKES TWENTY

INGREDIENTS
- 250g/9oz/2¼ cups self-raising (self-rising) flour
- 10ml/2 tsp bicarbonate of soda (baking soda)
- 50g/2oz/¼ cup caster (superfine) sugar
- 115g/4oz/½ cup unsalted (sweet) butter, diced
- finely grated rind of 1 large orange
- 115g/4oz/½ cup Greek honey
- 25g/1oz/¼ cup pine nuts or chopped walnuts

For the filling
- 50g/2oz/¼ cup unsalted (sweet) butter, at room temperature, diced
- 115g/4oz/1 cup icing (confectioners') sugar, sifted
- 15ml/1 tbsp Greek honey

1 Preheat the oven to 200°C/400°F/ Gas 6. Line three or four baking sheets with baking parchment. Sift the flour, bicarbonate of soda and caster sugar into a bowl. Add the butter and rub in until the mixture resembles breadcrumbs. Stir in the orange rind.

2 Put the honey in a small pan and heat until just runny but not hot. Pour over the dry mixture and mix to a firm dough.

3 Divide the dough in half and shape one half into 20 small balls about the size of a hazelnut in its shell. Place the balls on the baking sheets, spaced well apart, and gently flatten. Bake for 6–8 minutes, until golden brown. Leave to cool and firm up on the baking sheets. Use a palette knife or metal spatula to transfer the cookies to a wire rack to allow them to cool completely.

4 Shape the remaining dough into 20 balls and dip one side of each one into the pine nuts or walnuts. Place the cookies, nut sides up, on the baking sheets, gently flatten and bake for 6–8 minutes, until golden brown. Leave to cool and firm up slightly on the baking sheets before carefully transferring the cookies to a wire rack, still nut sides up, to cool completely.

5 To make the filling, put the butter, sugar and honey in a bowl and beat together until light and fluffy.

6 Use the honey and butter mixture to sandwich the cookies together in pairs. Spread a little filling on a plain cookie for the base and place a nut-coated one on top. Press the cookies together gently without squeezing out the filling.

Energy 164Kcal/688kJ; Protein 1.4g; Carbohydrate 23.5g, of which sugars 14.2g; Fat 7.8g, of which saturates 4.4g; Cholesterol 18mg; Calcium 47mg; Fibre 0.4g; Sodium 97mg.

LEMON TART

THIS CLASSIC FRENCH TART IS ONE OF THE MOST DELICIOUS DESSERTS. A RICH LEMON CURD IS
ENCASED IN A CRISP PASTRY CASE. CRÈME FRAÎCHE IS AN OPTIONAL — BUT NICE — EXTRA.

SERVES SIX

INGREDIENTS
  6 eggs, beaten
  350g/12oz/1½ cups caster
    (superfine) sugar
  115g/4oz/½ cup butter
  grated rind and juice of
    4 lemons
  icing (confectioners') sugar,
    for dusting
For the pastry
  225g/8oz/2 cups plain
    (all-purpose) flour
  115g/4oz/½ cup butter, diced
  30ml/2 tbsp icing
    (confectioners') sugar
  1 egg
  5ml/1 tsp vanilla extract
  15ml/1 tbsp chilled water

1 Preheat the oven to 200°C/400°F/
Gas 6. To make the pastry, sift the flour
into a mixing bowl and rub or cut in the
butter until the mixture resembles fine
breadcrumbs. Stir in the icing sugar.

2 Add the egg, vanilla and most of the
chilled water, then work to a soft dough.
Add a few more drops of water if needed.
Knead quickly and lightly until smooth.

3 Roll out the pastry on a floured
surface and use to line a 23cm/9in flan
tin (tart pan). Prick the base all over
with a fork. Line with baking parchment
and fill with baking beans. Bake in the
oven for 10 minutes. Remove the paper
and beans and set the pastry case (pie
shell) aside while you make the filling.

4 Put the eggs, sugar and butter into
a pan, and stir over a low heat until all
the sugar has dissolved. Add the lemon
rind and juice, and continue cooking,
stirring constantly, until the lemon curd
has thickened slightly.

5 Pour the curd mixture into the pastry
case. Bake for about 20 minutes, or
until the lemon curd filling is just set.
Transfer the tart to a wire rack to cool.
Dust the surface of the tart generously
with icing sugar just before serving.

Energy 623Kcal/2623kJ; Protein 12.7g; Carbohydrate 95.5g, of which sugars 66.8g; Fat 24g, of which saturates 12.2g; Cholesterol 307mg; Calcium 127mg; Fibre 1.2g; Sodium 219mg.

MADEIRA CAKE WITH LEMON SYRUP

THIS SUGAR-CRUSTED CAKE IS SOAKED IN LEMON SYRUP, SO IT STAYS MOIST AND IS INFUSED WITH TANGY CITRUS. SERVE IT SLICED WITH TEA FOR ONE OF THOSE "CARING AND SHARING" SESSIONS.

SERVES TEN

INGREDIENTS

- 250g/9oz/1 cup plus 2 tbsp butter, softened
- 225g/8oz/generous 1 cup caster (superfine) sugar
- 5 eggs
- 275g/10oz/2½ cups plain (all-purpose) flour, sifted
- 10ml/2 tsp baking powder
- salt

For the sugar crust
- 60ml/4 tbsp lemon juice
- 15ml/1 tbsp golden (light corn) syrup
- 30ml/2 tbsp granulated sugar

COOK'S TIP

Make double the quantity of cake. Omit the syrup from one and leave plain. Simply cool, wrap and freeze.

1 Preheat the oven to 180°C/350°F/Gas 4. Grease a 1kg/2¼lb loaf tin. Beat the butter and sugar until light and creamy, then gradually beat in the eggs.

2 Mix the sifted flour, baking powder and salt, and fold in gently. Spoon into the prepared tin, level the top and bake for 1¼ hours, until a skewer pushed into the middle comes out clean.

3 Remove the cake from the oven and, while still warm and in the tin, use a skewer to pierce it several times right the way through. Warm together the lemon juice and syrup, add the sugar and immediately spoon over the cake, so the flavoured syrup soaks through but leaves some sugar crystals on the top. Chill the cake for several hours or overnight before serving.

Energy 429Kcal/1796kJ; Protein 6.6g; Carbohydrate 49.4g, of which sugars 28.5g; Fat 24.2g, of which saturates 14g; Cholesterol 167mg; Calcium 74mg; Fibre 0.9g; Sodium 202mg.

PECAN CAKE

THIS CAKE IS AN EXAMPLE OF THE FRENCH INFLUENCE ON MEXICAN COOKING. IT IS TRADITIONALLY SERVED WITH CAJETA – SWEETENED BOILED MILK – BUT WHIPPED CREAM OR CRÈME FRAÎCHE CAN BE USED INSTEAD. SERVE THE CAKE WITH A FEW REDCURRANTS FOR A SPLASH OF UPLIFTING COLOUR.

SERVES EIGHT TO TEN

INGREDIENTS
 115g/4oz/1 cup pecan nuts
 115g/4oz/½ cup butter, softened
 115g/4oz/½ cup soft light
  brown sugar
 5ml/1 tsp vanilla extract
 4 large (US extra large) eggs,
  separated
 75g/3oz/¾ cup plain (all-purpose)
  flour
 pinch of salt
 12 whole pecan nuts, to decorate
 whipped cream or crème fraîche
For drizzling
 50g/2oz/¼ cup butter
 120ml/4fl oz/scant ½ cup clear honey

1 Preheat the oven to 180°C/350°F/ Gas 4. Grease a 20cm/8in round cake tin. Toast the nuts in a dry frying pan for 5 minutes, shaking frequently. Grind finely and place in a bowl.

2 Cream the butter with the sugar in a mixing bowl, then beat in the vanilla essence and egg yolks.

3 Add the flour to the ground nuts and mix well. Whisk the egg whites with the salt in a grease-free bowl until soft peaks form. Fold the whites into the butter mixture, then gently fold in the flour and nut mixture. Spoon the mixture into the prepared cake tin and bake for 30 minutes or until a skewer inserted in the centre comes out clean.

4 Cool the cake in the tin for 5 minutes, then remove the sides of the tin. Stand the cake on a wire rack until cold.

5 Remove the cake from the base of the tin if necessary, then return it to the rack and arrange the pecans on top. Transfer to a plate. Melt the butter in a small pan, add the honey and bring to the boil, stirring. Lower the heat and simmer for 3 minutes. Pour over the cake. Serve with whipped cream or crème fraîche.

Energy 428Kcal/1785kJ; Protein 6.2g; Carbohydrate 34.7g, of which sugars 27.4g; Fat 30.5g, of which saturates 12.5g; Cholesterol 158mg; Calcium 51mg; Fibre 1g; Sodium 170mg.

VICTORIA SANDWICH CAKE

SERVE THIS RICHLY FLAVOURED SPONGE CAKE SANDWICHED TOGETHER WITH YOUR FAVOURITE JAM OR PRESERVE. FOR SPECIAL OCCASIONS, FILL THE CAKE WITH PREPARED FRESH FRUIT, SUCH AS RASPBERRIES OR SLICED PEACHES, AS WELL AS JAM AND WHIPPED DAIRY CREAM OR FROMAGE FRAIS.

MAKES ONE 18CM/7IN CAKE

INGREDIENTS
175g/6oz/¾ cup soft butter
175g/6oz/¾ cup caster (superfine) sugar
3 eggs beaten
175g/6oz/1½ cups self-raising (self-rising) flour, sifted
60ml/4 tbsp jam (jelly)
150ml/¼pt/⅔ cup whipped cream or fromage frais
15–30ml/1–2 tbsp icing (confectioners') sugar, for dusting

3 Add the eggs, a little at a time, beating well after each addition. Fold in half the flour, using a metal spoon, then fold in the rest.

6 When the cakes are cool, sandwich them with the jam and whipped cream or fromage frais. Dust the top of the cake with sifted icing sugar and serve cut into slices. Store the cake in the refrigerator in an airtight container or wrapped in foil.

1 Preheat the oven to 180°C/350°F/ Gas 4. Lightly grease two 18cm/7in sandwich tins (layer cake pans) and line the base with baking parchment.

4 Divide the mixture between the two sandwich tins and level the surfaces with the back of a spoon.

VARIATIONS
• Replace 30ml/2 tbsp of the flour with sifted unsweetened cocoa powder. Sandwich the cakes with chocolate butter icing. For butter icing, beat 75g/3oz/6 tbsp softened butter or margarine, 225g/8oz/2 cups sifted icing sugar, 1 tbsp vanilla extract and 1 tbsp of milk together in a bowl, adding extra milk to give a light, smooth and fluffy consistency. For chocolate butter icing, blend 1 tbsp unsweetened cocoa powder with 1 tbsp hot water. Allow to cool before beating into the icing. For a darker richer, chocolate cake, add 90ml/6 tbsp cocoa powder without reducing the quantity of flour.
• To make a moist coffee cake, dissolve 15ml/1 tbsp instant coffee in 30ml/ 2 tbsp boiling water and fold this in at the end, when the flour has been incorporated. Sandwich together with a coffee butter icing or with cream whipped with a little dissolved instant coffee and sweetened with icing sugar. For coffee butter icing, blend 2 tsp instant coffee powder or granules with 1 tbsp boiling water. Allow to cool before beating into the icing.

2 Place the butter and caster sugar in a bowl and cream together until pale and fluffy.

5 Bake for 25–30 minutes, until the cakes have risen, feel just firm to the touch and are golden brown. Turn out and cool on a wire rack.

COOK'S TIP
The butter and sugar mixture can be creamed using a hand-held electric mixer or in a food processor.

Energy 3553Kcal/14845kJ; Protein 42.5g; Carbohydrate 362.6g, of which sugars 232.5g; Fat 225.3g, of which saturates 43.8g; Cholesterol 842mg; Calcium 908mg; Fibre 5.4g; Sodium 2358mg.

FROSTED CARROT AND PARSNIP CAKE

THE GRATED CARROTS AND PARSNIPS IN THIS DELICIOUSLY LIGHT AND CRUMBLY CAKE HELP TO KEEP IT MOIST AND ACCOUNT FOR ITS VERY GOOD KEEPING QUALITIES. THE CREAMY SWEETNESS OF THE COOKED MERINGUE TOPPING MAKES A WONDERFUL CONTRAST TO THE CAKE'S LIGHT CRUMB.

SERVES EIGHT TO TEN

INGREDIENTS
   oil, for greasing
   1 lemon
   1 orange
   15ml/1 tbsp caster (superfine) sugar
   225g/8oz/1 cup butter
   225g/8oz/1 cup soft light brown
      sugar
   4 eggs
   225g/8oz/1⅔ cups carrot and
      parsnip, grated
   115g/4oz/1¼ cups sultanas (golden
      raisins)
   225g/8oz/2 cups self-raising (self-
      rising) wholemeal (whole-wheat)
      flour
   5ml/1 tsp baking powder
For the topping
   50g/2oz/¼ cup caster (superfine)
      sugar
   1 egg white

1 Preheat the oven to 180°C/350°F/ Gas 4. Lightly grease a 20cm/8in loose-based cake tin and line the base with a circle of greaseproof paper.

VARIATION
If you do not like parsnips, you can make this cake with just carrots, or replace the parsnips with the same weight of shredded courgettes. Add a pinch of cinnamon and nutmeg to the mixture to give a little extra flavour.

2 Finely grate the lemon and orange rind. Put about half of the rind, selecting the longest shreds, in a bowl and mix with the caster sugar. Arrange the sugar-coated rind on a sheet of baking parchment and leave in a warm place, to dry thoroughly.

3 Cream the butter and sugar until pale and fluffy. Add the eggs gradually, then beat well. Stir in the unsugared rinds, the grated carrots and parsnips, 30ml/ 2 tbsp orange juice and the sultanas.

4 Gradually fold in the flour and baking powder, and tip into the prepared tin. Bake for 1½ hours until risen, golden and just firm.

5 Leave the cake to cool slightly in the tin, then turn out on to a serving plate.

6 To make the topping, place the caster sugar in a bowl over boiling water with 30ml/2 tbsp of the remaining orange juice. Stir over the heat until the sugar begins to dissolve. Remove from the heat, add the egg white and salt, and whisk for 1 minute with an electric beater.

7 Return to the heat and whisk for about 6 minutes until the mixture becomes stiff and glossy, holding a good shape. Allow to cool slightly, whisking frequently.

8 Swirl the cooked meringue topping over the cake and leave to firm up for about 1 hour. To serve, sprinkle with the sugared lemon and orange rind, which should now be dry and crumbly.

COOK'S TIP
When this cooked meringue frosting cools, it becomes slightly hard on the outside. The cake will keep well for a few days until the crust is cut into.

Energy 540Kcal/2265kJ; Protein 7.5g; Carbohydrate 71.5g, of which sugars 50.5g; Fat 26.9g, of which saturates 15.7g; Cholesterol 174mg; Calcium 156mg; Fibre 1.8g; Sodium 333mg.

MOIST APPLE CAKE

THIS DELICIOUS CAKE IS PERHAPS BEST IN AUTUMN, WHEN HOME-GROWN APPLES ARE IN SEASON. IT HAS A LOVELY CRUNCHY TOP AND CAN BE SERVED COLD, AS A CAKE, OR WARM WITH CHILLED CREAM OR CUSTARD AS A DESSERT.

MAKES ONE 20CM/8IN CAKE

INGREDIENTS
225g/8oz/2 cups self-raising
  (self-rising) flour
good pinch of salt
pinch of ground cloves
115g/4oz/1/2 cup butter,
  at room temperature
4 cooking apples
115g/4oz/generous 1/2 cup caster
  (superfine) sugar
2 eggs, beaten
a little milk to mix
granulated sugar to sprinkle over

1 Preheat the oven to 190°C/375°F/ Gas 5 and butter a 20cm/8in round cake tin (pan).

2 Sift the flour, salt and ground cloves into a bowl. Cut in the butter and rub in until the mixture is like fine breadcrumbs. Peel and core the apples. Slice them thinly and add to the rubbed in mixture with the sugar.

3 Mix in the eggs and enough milk to make a fairly stiff dough, then turn the mixture into the prepared tin and sprinkle with granulated sugar.

4 Bake in the preheated oven for 30–40 minutes, or until springy to the touch. Cool on a wire rack. When cold store in an airtight container until ready to serve.

Energy 2315Kcal/9717kJ; Protein 37g; Carbohydrate 312.5g, of which sugars 145.3g; Fat 110.9g, of which saturates 64.1g; Cholesterol 702mg; Calcium 948mg; Fibre 10.7g; Sodium 1.68g.

ORANGE CHOCOLATE LOAF

DO NOT BE ALARMED AT THE AMOUNT OF CREAM IN THIS RECIPE — IT'S NAUGHTY BUT NECESSARY, AND REPLACES BUTTER TO MAKE A DELICIOUSLY MOUTHWATERING, MOIST AND DARK CHOCOLATE CAKE. A BITTERSWEET STICKY MARMALADE FILLING AND TOPPING IS THE PERFECT FINISH.

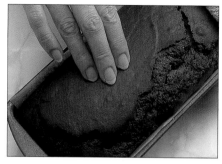

4 Pour the mixture into the prepared tin and bake for about 1 hour, or until well risen and firm to the touch. Cool for a few minutes in the tin, then turn out on to a wire rack and let the loaf cool completely.

5 Make the filling. Spoon two-thirds of the marmalade into a small pan and melt over a low heat. Break the chocolate into pieces. Melt the chocolate in a heatproof bowl placed over hot water. Stir the chocolate into the marmalade with the sour cream.

6 Slice the cake across into three layers and sandwich back together with about half the marmalade filling. Spread the rest over the top of the cake and leave to set. Spoon the remaining marmalade over the cake and scatter with shredded orange rind, to decorate.

COOK'S TIP
A fantastic variety of different types of organic marmalades is available, including farmhouse and hand-made regional varieties.

SERVES EIGHT

INGREDIENTS
115g/4oz dark (bittersweet) chocolate
3 eggs
175g/6oz/scant 1 cup unrefined caster (superfine) sugar
175ml/6fl oz/¾ cup sour cream
200g/7oz/1¾ cups self-raising (self-rising) flour
For the filling and topping
200g/7oz/⅔ cup bitter orange marmalade
115g/4oz dark (bittersweet) chocolate
60ml/4 tbsp sour cream
shredded orange rind, to decorate

1 Preheat the oven to 190°C/375°F/Gas 5. Grease a 900g/2lb loaf tin (pan) lightly, then line the base with a piece of baking parchment.

2 Break the chocolate into pieces and place them in a heatproof bowl. Stand this over a pan of hot, not boiling, water and stir until melted.

3 Combine the eggs and sugar in a separate bowl. Using a hand-held electric mixer, beat the mixture until it is thick and creamy, then stir in the sour cream and melted chocolate. Fold in the flour evenly using a metal spoon.

Energy 474Kcal/1998kJ; Protein 7.5g; Carbohydrate 78.5g, of which sugars 59.7g; Fat 16.7g, of which saturates 9.3g; Cholesterol 105mg; Calcium 155mg; Fibre 1.6g; Sodium 153mg.

CHELSEA BUNS

SAID TO HAVE BEEN INVENTED BY THE OWNER OF THE CHELSEA BUN HOUSE IN LONDON AT THE END OF THE 17TH CENTURY, CHELSEA BUNS MAKE THE PERFECT ACCOMPANIMENT TO A CUP OF COFFEE OR TEA. THEY ARE SO DELICIOUS, IT IS DIFFICULT TO RESIST EATING SEVERAL IN ONE SITTING!

MAKES TWELVE

INGREDIENTS
   500g/1lb 2oz/4½ cups unbleached
     strong white bread flour
   2.5ml/½ tsp salt
   50g/2oz/¼ cup butter, softened
   75g/3oz/6 tbsp caster (superfine)
     sugar
   5ml/1tsp easy-blend (rapid rise)
     dried yeast
   225ml/8fl oz/scant 1 cup hand-hot
     milk
   1 egg, beaten
For the glaze
   50g/2oz/¼ cup caster (superfine)
     sugar
   5ml/1 tsp orange flower water
For the filling
   25g/1oz/2 tbsp butter, melted
   115g/4oz/⅔ cup sultanas
     (golden raisins)
   25g/1oz/3 tbsp mixed chopped
     (candied) peel
   25g/1oz/2 tbsp currants
   25g/1oz/2 tbsp soft light brown sugar
   5ml/1 tsp mixed (apple pie) spice

1 Mix the flour and salt in a large bowl, then rub in the butter and stir in the sugar and yeast.

2 Make a well in the middle of the dry ingredients and add the milk and egg. Mix the liquids into the dry ingredients to make a firm dough.

3 Turn the dough out on to a floured surface and knead thoroughly for about 10 minutes, until it is smooth and elastic. Flour the mixing bowl, return the dough to it and cover with oiled clear film (plastic wrap). Leave in a warm place until doubled in size.

4 Lightly grease a 23cm/9in square cake tin (pan). When the dough has risen, turn it out on to a floured surface and knock it back (punch it down).

5 Roll out the dough on a lightly floured surface into a square that measures about 30cm/12in.

6 Brush the dough with the melted butter for the filling and sprinkle it with the sultanas, mixed peel, currants, brown sugar and mixed spice, leaving a 1cm/½in border along one edge.

7 Starting at a covered edge, roll the dough up, Swiss (jelly) roll fashion. Press the edges together to seal. Cut the roll into 12 slices and then place these cut side uppermost in the prepared tin.

8 Cover with oiled clear film. Leave the buns to rise in a warm place for about 30–45 minutes, or until the dough slices have doubled in size and are almost at the top of the tin.

9 Meanwhile, preheat the oven to 200°C/400°F/Gas 6. Bake the buns for 15–20 minutes, or until they have risen well and are evenly golden all over.

10 Once they are baked, leave the buns to cool slightly in the tin before lifting them out and transferring them to a wire rack to cool.

11 Gently heat the ingredients for the glaze in a small pan until the sugar is dissolved. Brush the mixture over the warm buns. Serve slightly warm.

VARIATION
Use icing (confectioners') sugar instead of caster sugar and make a thin glaze icing to brush or trickle over the freshly baked buns.

MALTED CURRANT BREAD

THIS SPICED CURRANT BREAD MAKES A GOOD TEA OR BREAKFAST BREAD, SLICED AND SPREAD WITH A GENEROUS AMOUNT OF BUTTER. IT ALSO MAKES SUPERB TOAST FOR A MIDNIGHT SNACK.

MAKES TWO LOAVES

INGREDIENTS
   50g/2oz/3 tbsp malt extract
   30ml/2 tbsp golden (light corn) syrup
   50g/2oz/¼ cup butter
   450g/1lb/4 cups unbleached strong
     white bread flour
   5ml/1 tsp mixed (apple pie) spice
   20g/¾ oz fresh yeast
   175ml/6fl oz/¾ cup lukewarm milk
   175g/6oz/¾ cup currants,
     slightly warmed
For the glaze
   30ml/2 tbsp milk
   30ml/2 tbsp caster (superfine) sugar

1 Lightly grease two 450g/1lb loaf tins (pans). Place the malt extract, golden syrup and butter in a pan and heat gently until the butter has melted. Set aside to cool completely.

2 Sift the flour and mixed spice together into a large bowl and make a well in the centre. Cream the yeast with a little of the milk, then blend in the remaining milk. Add the yeast mixture and cooled malt mixture to the centre of the flour and blend together to form a dough.

3 Turn out the dough on to a lightly floured surface and knead for about 10 minutes until smooth and elastic. Place in a lightly oiled bowl, cover with lightly oiled clear film (plastic wrap) and leave to rise, in a warm place, for 1½–2 hours, or until doubled in bulk.

4 Turn the dough out on to a lightly floured surface, knock back (punch down), then knead in the currants. Divide the dough in two and shape into two loaves. Place in the prepared tins. Cover with oiled clear film and leave to rise, in a warm place, for 2–3 hours, or until the dough reaches the top of the tins.

5 Meanwhile, preheat the oven to 200ºC/400ºF/Gas 6. Bake for 35–40 minutes or until golden. While the loaves are baking heat the milk and sugar for the glaze in a small pan. Turn out the loaves on to a wire rack, then invert them, so that they are the right way up. Immediately brush the glaze evenly over the loaves and leave to cool.

COOK'S TIP
When you are making more than one loaf, the easiest way to prove (rise) them is to place the tins in a lightly oiled large plastic bag.

Energy 1336Kcal/5659kJ; Protein 26.7g; Carbohydrate 267.1g, of which sugars 95.5g; Fat 25.3g, of which saturates 14.4g; Cholesterol 58mg; Calcium 646mg; Fibre 8.7g; Sodium 294mg.

FRUITLOAF

DRIED FRUIT AND FLAKED ALMONDS ARE DELICIOUS IN THIS ENERGY-GIVING SWEET BREAD. SERVE IT THICKLY SLICED AND SPREAD WITH GOOD BUTTER TO REPLENISH SPENT ENERGY. IT IS A GREAT LOAF FOR WEEKEND BREAKFASTS, ESPECIALLY AFTER A LATE NIGHT, AND A GOOD CHOICE FOR AFTERNOON TEA WHEN THE CHILDREN COME HOME WITH RAGING APPETITES.

SERVES EIGHT TO TEN

INGREDIENTS
   sunflower oil, for greasing
   7 egg whites
   175g/6oz/scant 1 cup caster
      (superfine) sugar
   115g/4oz/1 cup flaked (sliced)
      almonds, toasted
   115g/4oz/¾ cup sultanas (golden
      raisins)
   grated rind of 1 lemon
   165g/5½oz/1⅓ cups plain
      (all-purpose) flour, sifted, plus extra
      for flouring
   75g/3oz/6 tbsp butter, melted

1 Preheat the oven to 180°C/350°F/ Gas 4 and grease and flour a 1kg/2¼lb loaf tin (pan). Whisk the egg whites until they are very stiff, but not crumbly. Fold in the sugar gradually, then add the almonds, sultanas and lemon rind.

2 Fold the flour and butter into the mixture and turn it into the prepared tin. Bake for about 45 minutes until well risen and pale golden brown. Cool for a few minutes in the tin, then turn out and serve warm or cold, in slices.

Energy 364Kcal/1529kJ; Protein 8.1g; Carbohydrate 49.9g, of which sugars 33.8g; Fat 16.1g, of which saturates 5.6g; Cholesterol 20mg; Calcium 87mg; Fibre 2g; Sodium 117mg.

PANETTONE

THIS CLASSIC ITALIAN BREAD CAN BE FOUND THROUGHOUT ITALY AROUND CHRISTMAS. IT IS A SURPRISINGLY LIGHT BREAD EVEN THOUGH IT IS RICH WITH BUTTER AND DRIED FRUIT.

MAKES ONE LOAF

INGREDIENTS
  400g/14oz/3½ cups unbleached
    strong white bread flour
  2.5ml/½ tsp salt
  15g/½ oz fresh yeast
  120ml/4fl oz/½ cup lukewarm milk
  2 eggs plus 2 egg yolks
  75g/3oz/6 tbsp caster (superfine)
    sugar
  150g/5oz/⅔ cup butter, softened
  115g/4oz/⅔ cup mixed chopped
    (candied) peel
  75g/3oz/½ cup raisins
  melted butter, for brushing

COOK'S TIP
Once the dough has been enriched with butter, do not prove (rise) in too warm a place or the loaf will become greasy.

1 Using a double layer of baking parchment, line and butter a 15cm/6in deep cake tin (pan) or soufflé dish. Finish the paper 7.5cm/3in above the top of the tin.

2 Sift the flour and salt together into a large bowl. Make a well in the centre. Cream the yeast with 60ml/4 tbsp of the milk, then mix in the remainder.

3 Pour the yeast mixture into the centre of the flour, add the whole eggs and mix in sufficient flour to make a thick batter. Sprinkle a little of the remaining flour over the top and leave to "sponge", in a warm place, for 30 minutes.

4 Add the egg yolks and sugar and mix to a soft dough. Work in the softened butter, then turn out on to a lightly floured surface and knead for 5 minutes until smooth and elastic. Place in a lightly oiled bowl, cover with lightly oiled clear film (plastic wrap) and leave to rise, in a slightly warm place, for 1½–2 hours, or until doubled in bulk.

5 Knock back (punch down) the dough and turn out on to a lightly floured surface. Gently knead in the peel and raisins. Shape into a ball and place in the prepared tin. Cover with lightly oiled clear film and leave to rise, in a slightly warm place, for about 1 hour, or until doubled.

6 Meanwhile, preheat the oven to 190°C/375°F/Gas 5. Brush the surface with melted butter and cut a cross in the top using a sharp knife. Bake for 20 minutes, then reduce the oven temperature to 180°C/350°F/Gas 4. Brush the top with butter again and bake for a further 25–30 minutes, or until golden. Cool in the tin for 5–10 minutes, then turn out on to a wire rack to cool.

Energy 3599Kcal/15123kJ; Protein 65.7g; Carbohydrate 515.7g, of which sugars 210.9g; Fat 156.2g, of which saturates 87.1g; Cholesterol 1187mg; Calcium 1070mg; Fibre 19.4g; Sodium 1530mg.

LARDY CAKE

THIS SPECIAL RICH FRUIT BREAD WAS ORIGINALLY MADE THROUGHOUT MANY COUNTIES OF ENGLAND FOR CELEBRATING THE HARVEST. USING LARD RATHER THAN BUTTER OR MARGARINE MAKES AN AUTHENTIC LARDY CAKE. IT IS FLAKY, RICH AND JUST WHAT THE DOCTOR ORDERED FOR CHEERING UP.

MAKES ONE LARGE LOAF

INGREDIENTS
   450g/1lb/4 cups unbleached strong
      white bread flour
   5ml/1 tsp salt
   15g/½oz/1 tbsp lard (shortening)
   25g/1oz/2 tbsp caster (superfine)
      sugar
   20g/¾oz fresh yeast
   300ml/½ pint/1¼ cups lukewarm
      water
For the filling
   75g/3oz/6 tbsp lard (shortening)
   75g/3oz/6 tbsp soft light brown sugar
   115g/4oz/½ cup currants,
      slightly warmed
   75g/3oz/½ cup sultanas (golden
      raisins), slightly warmed
   25g/1oz/3 tbsp mixed chopped
      (candied) peel
   5ml/1 tsp mixed (apple pie) spice
For the glaze
   10ml/2 tsp sunflower oil
   15–30ml/1–2 tbsp caster (superfine)
      sugar

1 Grease a 25 x 20cm/10 x 8in shallow roasting pan. Sift the flour and salt into a large bowl and rub in the lard. Stir in the sugar and make a well in the centre.

2 In a bowl, cream the yeast with half of the water, then blend in the remainder. Add to the centre of the flour and mix to a smooth dough.

3 Turn out on to a lightly floured surface and knead for 10 minutes until smooth and elastic. Place in a lightly oiled bowl, cover with oiled clear film (plastic wrap) and leave in a warm place for 1 hour, or until doubled in bulk.

4 Turn the dough out on to a lightly floured surface and knock back (punch down) until collapsed. Knead for 2–3 minutes. Roll into a rectangle about 5mm/¼in thick.

5 Using half the lard for the filling, cover the top two-thirds of the dough with flakes of lard. Sprinkle over half the sugar, half the dried fruits and peel and half the mixed spice. Fold the bottom third up and the top third down, sealing the edges with the rolling pin.

6 Turn the dough by 90 degrees. Repeat the rolling and cover with the remaining lard, fruit and peel and mixed spice. Fold, seal and turn as before. Roll out the dough to fit the prepared pan. Cover with lightly oiled clear film and leave to rise, in a warm place, for 30–45 minutes, or until doubled in size.

7 Meanwhile, preheat the oven to 200°C/400°F/Gas 6. Brush the top of the lardy cake with sunflower oil and sprinkle with caster sugar.

8 Score a criss-cross pattern on top using a sharp knife, then bake for 30–40 minutes until golden. Turn out on to a wire rack to cool slightly. Serve warm, cut into slices or squares.

Energy 3474Kcal/14663kJ; Protein 47.7g; Carbohydrate 630.3g, of which sugars 287.4g; Fat 101.9g, of which saturates 37.9g; Cholesterol 84mg; Calcium 888mg; Fibre 18.8g; Sodium 2080mg.

INDEX

almond and lemon tart 55
almond and raspberry trifle 12
almond, pear and ground rice
    pie 39
apple cake 88
apple charlotte 25
apple crumble 33
apple pie 32
apricot panettone pudding 38

baked bananas with ice
    cream 51
baked caramel custard 22
baked maple and pecan croissant
    pudding 42
Bakewell tart 54
blackberry charlotte 34
Boston banoffee pie 27
brandied apple charlotte 25
bread
    Chelsea buns 90–1
    lardy cake 95
    malted currant bread 92
    panettone 94
bread and butter pudding with
    whiskey sauce 36

cakes
    brandied apple charlotte 25
    chocolate potato cake 74–5
    frosted carrot and parsnip
        cake 86–7
    fruitloaf 93
    Madeira cake with lemon
        syrup 82
    pecan cake 83
    Victoria sandwich cake 84–5
caramel custard 22
caramel custards, citrus 45
carrot and parsnip cake 86–7
Chelsea buns 90–1
chewy flapjack bars 70
chocolate
    chocolate cheesecake 16
    chocolate cheesecake
        brownies 76
    chocolate éclairs 78–9
    chocolate mousse cups 20
    chocolate potato cake
        74–5
    chocolate pudding with rum
        custard 46
    chocolate ripple ice cream 11
    chocolate, rum and raisin
        roulade 13

frothy hot chocolate 59
giant triple chocolate
    cookies 73
Irish chocolate velvet 61
Mississippi mud pie 26
oaty chocolate-chip
    cookies 72
orange chocolate loaf 89
white chocolate brownies 77
cinnamon rings 68
citrus and caramel custards 45
classic vanilla ice cream 10
coconut rice pudding 44
coffee
    coffee egg-nog 61
    pecan toffee shortbread 71
    sticky coffee and ginger
        pudding 47
    vanilla caffè latte 58
cookies
    giant triple chocolate cookies
        73
    Greek honey crunch
        creams 80
    oaty chocolate-chip
        cookies 72
crêpes with orange sauce 30–1
croissants 66
custards
    baked caramel custard 22
    chocolate pudding with rum
        custard 46
    custard 45

Danish pastries 64
deep-dish apple pie 32
drinks
    coffee egg-nog 61
    frothy hot chocolate 59
    hot toddy 60
    Irish chocolate velvet 61
    vanilla caffè latte 58

flapjack bars 70
fresh currant bread and butter
    pudding 49
frosted carrot and parsnip
    cake 86–7
frothy hot chocolate 59
fruit
    blackberry charlotte 34
    crêpes with orange sauce
        30–1
    deep-dish apple pie 32
    fresh currant bread and butter
        pudding 49
    iced raspberry and almond
        trifle 12
    Key lime pie 19
    lemon and almond tart 55
    lemon cheesecake with forest
        fruits 17
    lemon meringue pie 18
    lemon tart 81
    orange chocolate loaf 89
    orange whisky butter with
        mince pies 56–7
    pear, almond and ground rice
        pie 39

raspberry mousse gâteau 21
spiced apple crumble 33
spiced pears with nut
    crumble 37
summer pudding 24
fruitloaf 93

giant triple chocolate
    cookies 73
Greek honey crunch creams 80

hot toddy 60

ice cream
    baked bananas with ice
        cream 51
    chocolate ripple ice cream 10
    classic vanilla ice cream 11
    zabaglione ice cream torte 14
iced raspberry and almond
    trifle 12
iced tiramisù 15
Irish chocolate velvet 61

Key lime pie 19

lardy cake 953
lime pie 19

Madeira cake with lemon
    syrup 82
mince pies with orange whisky
    butter 56–7
Mississippi mud pie 26
moist apple cake 88

nuts
    giant triple chocolate
        cookies 73
    iced raspberry and almond
        trifle 12
    lemon and almond tart 55
    pecan cake 83
    pecan coffee shortbread 71
    spiced pears with nut
        crumble 37

oaty chocolate-chip cookies 72

panettone 94
panettone pudding, apricot 38
parsnip and carrot cake 86–7
pastry
    Bakewell tart 54
    Boston banoffee pie 27
    chocolate éclairs 78–9
    deep-dish apple pie 32
    Key lime pie 19
    lemon and almond tart 55
    lemon meringue pie 18
    lemon tart 81
    mince pies with orange whisky
        butter 56–7
    Mississippi mud pie 26
    treacle tart 53
    Yorkshire curd tart 52
pecan and maple croissant
    pudding 42
pecan cake 83

pecan toffee shortbread 71
plum charlottes with foamy
    Kirsch sauce 40
puddings
    apricot panettone pudding 38
    baked maple and pecan
        croissant pudding 42
    chocolate pudding with rum
        custard 46
    fresh currant bread and butter
        pudding 49
    sticky coffee and ginger
        pudding 47
    sticky toffee pudding 48
    summer pudding 24

rice
    almond, pear and ground
        rice pie 39
    coconut rice pudding 44
    traditional English rice
        pudding 50
rum custard with chocolate
    pudding 46
rum, raisin and chocolate
    roulade 13

spiced pears with nut
    crumble 37
sticky coffee and ginger
    pudding 47
sticky toffee pudding 48
summer pudding 24

tarts
    Bakewell tart 54
    lemon and almond tart 55
    treacle tart 53
    Yorkshire curd tart 52
tiramisù 15
traditional English rice
    pudding 50
treacle tart 53

vanilla caffè latte 58
vanilla ice cream 10
Victoria sandwich cake 84–5

whisky orange butter with mince
    pies 56–7
white chocolate brownies 77

Yorkshire curd tart 52

zabaglione ice cream torte 14